FROM
A to Z
to NARNIA

with C. S. Lewis

by LOUIS MARKOS

LAMPION
Press

From A to Z to Narnia with C.S. Lewis
Copyright © 2015 Louis Markos,
All rights reserved.

Lampion Press, LLC
P. O. Box 932
Silverton, OR 97381

All Scripture quotations, unless otherwise indicated, are taken from the Holy Bible, New International Version®, NIV®. Copyright ©1973, 1978, 1984, 2011 by Biblica, Inc.™ Used by permission of Zondervan. All rights reserved worldwide. www.zondervan.com The "NIV" and "New International Version" are trademarks registered in the United States Patent and Trademark Office by Biblica, Inc.™

Cover photograph by Arthur P. Strong (1947)

ISBN: 978-1-942614-04-3

Library of Congress Control Number: 2015944036

Cover design by Amy Cole, JPL Design Solutions

For Bobby, Martha, David, and Esther Mathew

Dear Friends

Ministry Partners

Co-Laborers in the Field

TABLE OF CONTENTS

INTRODUCTION

Professor, apologist, novelist, literary critic, fantasy writer, philosopher, theologian, and ethicist, C. S. Lewis has exerted a profound influence on the way millions of people read literature, make moral choices, think about God, and live out the Christian faith. By means of a genial blend of reason and imagination, logic and fantasy, profound academic insight and good old common sense, Lewis has challenged the modern world to re-examine the claims of Christ, the Bible, and the Church; re-experience the goodness, truth, and beauty of literature; and re-expand its vision of God, man, and the universe.

I, for one, would be a different person had C. S. Lewis never lived. He has inspired and shaped my thinking on such a wide range of topics that no single book could hope to capture the myriad ways in which he has tested my assumptions, altered my opinions, and refined my beliefs. And what he has done for me, he has done for tens of thousands of others across the globe.

To read Lewis is to engage in a sort of mental gymnastics. One simply cannot read his work passively or in a state of indifference. Knowledge for Lewis was not an end-in-itself, but a means to draw us closer to the truth about ourselves, our world, and our Creator. Though Lewis wrote more non-fiction than fiction, everything he wrote was informed by that Great Story of Creation, Fall, Redemption, and Restoration in which we all have a part to play; whether we want to or not. For Lewis, Christianity was first and foremost a story, a myth even; but it was a True Myth, a Real Story played out in historical time and space.

In this book, I shall explore some of the dimensions of that Universal Story by taking as my guide the wisdom, passion, and irrepressible creativity of C. S. Lewis. Like Plato and Dante before him, the depth and breadth of Lewis's vision took in every aspect of the human journey toward Meaning, Purpose, and Consummation. There can be no greater mentor, escort, and spiritual director than Lewis for the pilgrim who would find his way on that long road that stretches from Eden to the New Jerusalem.

I shall take my own pilgrimage in two stages. First, I will consider twenty-six separate topics of perennial interest to humanity and of particular interest to the early twenty-first century. These topics will range from Beauty to Courage, Desire to Faith, Love to Pain, Kingship to War. They will draw on the full range of Lewis's creative output: from *Mere Christianity* to The Chronicles of Narnia, *The Screwtape Letters* to *The Great Divorce*, *The Discarded Image* to *A Preface to Paradise Lost*, *The Problem of Pain* to *Miracles*, The Space Trilogy to *The Abolition of Man*.

The second stage will consist of three lengthy reviews of the film versions of *The Lion, the Witch and the Wardrobe*, *Prince Caspian*, and *The Voyage of the Dawn Treader*. Rather than over-praise the films for their cinematic power or over-condemn them for straying from the books, these reviews seek to assess those aspects of the films that draw out, and even improve on, elements of the novels, and those that, sadly, fail to capture the deeper dimensions of Lewis's deceptively simple fairy tales. In assessing those failures, I have extended grace to the filmmakers, suggesting that their deviations from the novels do not represent a conscious attempt to strip Narnia of its Christian dimensions but an inability to understand those dimensions. Indeed, my main purpose for including these reviews along with my A to Z entries is to further explore the nature of that Universal Story (or meta-narrative) that lies at the core of everything that Lewis wrote.

A biographical sketch and timeline of Lewis's life, an annotated bibliography of books by and about Lewis, and a reading list of books that should prove of interest to lovers of Narnia will round out the collection. With the exception of the biographical sketch, timeline, and bibliography, all parts of this book have appeared previously in a number of different journals.

The A to Z entries have appeared, in two installments, in the Winter 2013 and Summer 2013 issues of *The City*. My reviews of *The Lion, the Witch and the Wardrobe*; *Prince Caspian*; and *The Voyage of the Dawn Treader* have appeared, respectively, in the Spring 2006 issue of the *Bulletin of the New York C. S. Lewis Society*, Volume 6, Issue 1 (Winter 2009), the *Chronicle of the Oxford University C. S. Lewis Society*, and the March/April 2011 issue of *Saint Austin Review* (StAR). Finally, "Reading in the Shadow of Narnia" has appeared in the Spring 2012 (XXXII.3) issue of the *New Mexico Journal of Reading*. I offer my thanks to all of these journals.

Though he has been dead for over half a century, Lewis continues to beckon us to follow him along the road toward redemption and restoration. I invite you to join me as I journey in his footsteps.

C. S. LEWIS:
A BIOGRAPHICAL SKETCH

Clive Staples Lewis (known to his friends as Jack) was born on November 29, 1898, in Belfast, Ireland. Queen Victoria was on the throne, the British Empire was at her height, and Ireland had yet to be torn in two. Turbulent years were to follow—both for Lewis and for the British Isles—but none of that was evident in the decade following his birth.

Indeed, Lewis lived something of a charmed childhood. In 1905, he moved with his parents and older brother, Warnie (born in 1895), to a splendid old house filled with long, drafty corridors that stirred the fertile imaginations of the Lewis brothers. In one of the upstairs rooms, Jack and Warnie discovered a large wardrobe; in the years that followed, they would sit inside that wardrobe and invent made-up lands populated with dressed animals and the exotic locales of India.

When, in his fifties, Lewis wrote his spiritual autobiography (*Surprised by Joy*), he would recall from that glorious decade a series of mystical moments in which he felt transported from this world into a higher one. Those moments were generally set off by something that, on the surface, seemed quite ordinary: a toy garden made out of moss and twigs; a picture in a book by Beatrix Potter; a stray line of poetry about the Norse god Balder. Still, despite the humble nature of the object, Jack's encounter with it filled him with a sudden and overwhelming desire for something that transcended our mundane world of time and space.

Lewis's early spiritual growth was, in many ways, guided by these moments of joy, and, in the normal course of events, he would likely have blossomed into a teenager with a strong Christian faith. But that was not to be. In 1908, while Lewis was still in his ninth year of life, his beloved mother died of cancer. To complicate and exacerbate the blow, Lewis's father, rather than draw his distraught son closer to his bosom, packed him off to a series of British boarding schools that Lewis hated. When Lewis's youthful prayers proved incapable of saving his mother or bringing him back home, he began a slow process of detaching himself from the faith of his father and of his childhood.

Much needed relief from boarding school finally came in 1914, but it was a relief that ended up strengthening, rather than weakening, his growing atheism. For the next two years, Lewis studied under an empiricist tutor named Kirkpatrick who taught his impressionable young student to trust only logic, matter, and his senses. Lewis eventually came to believe that religion, though not necessarily evil, was irrelevant to the problems of the modern world.

And yet, even here, in the midst of his rejection of the supernatural and the metaphysical, Lewis was visited by an unexpected moment of joy. While returning to Ireland from Kirkpatrick's home in Surrey, England, Lewis, quite at random, picked up a copy of George MacDonald's novel, *Phantastes*, from a bookstall. The novel drew Lewis into a kind of fantasy world that he thought had been done away with by Kirkpatrick's militant naturalism. As he followed MacDonald into a strange, indefinable realm alive with divine presence, he came face to face with holiness. Reading the novel, Lewis would later write, baptized his imagination. Although it would take another decade and a half for the rest of him to follow suit, the process of opening his heart and soul to realities unaccounted for by Kirkpatrick's empiricism had begun.

Lewis's father had sent his son to Kirkpatrick for one express purpose: to prepare him for the entrance exams to the University of Oxford. The gamble worked, and Lewis became one of Oxford's finest students, though his education was interrupted by service in the First World War, during which time he was wounded by friendly fire. Eventually, Lewis became a fellow of Magdalen College, Oxford, where he served from 1925-54. Together with his brother and Mrs. Moore (the mother of one of Lewis's deceased war buddies, to whom Lewis had made a pledge to care for his mother if anything happened to him), Lewis purchased a home in Oxford known as the Kilns.

During his early years at Magdalen, Lewis continued to be a convinced atheist and materialist: that is, until his books and his friends began to turn against him. To his great surprise, the somewhat smug Lewis came to realize that all the authors he most loved (Dante, Edmund Spenser, John Donne, George Herbert, John Milton, Samuel Johnson, G. K. Chesterton) shared that very Christian faith that he had rejected as out of date. Meanwhile, those writers who shared his secular humanist worldview (John Stuart Mill, George Bernard Shaw, H. G. Wells, D. H. Lawrence) seemed to him oddly hollow. To make matters worse, the men he came most to respect at Oxford turned out to be infected by Christianity.

The last straw came when his friend Owen Barfield embraced the faith and began to take Lewis to task for being too quick to dismiss Christianity. Indeed, he accused Lewis of chronological snobbery, of taking for granted that because the doctrines and miracles of the Church were no longer believed by "cultured" people that they must have been disproved. Barfield's challenge forced Lewis to rethink medieval Christendom and led him, sometime in 1929 or 1930, to embrace theism. Lewis did so with great reluctance. He did not want to believe, yet he felt compelled by the evidence to bow his knee and confess God as God.

But he was not yet a Christian. Yes, he believed in God, but he found it difficult to accept that an obscure rabbi in first-century Palestine was the Son of God. Lewis, a student of comparative mythology, knew, from his reading of Sir James Frazer's *The Golden Bough*, that the ancient world abounded with stories of dying and rising gods: Osiris, Adonis, Mithras, Balder, and so forth. Was not Jesus of Nazareth merely the Hebrew version of this common archetype?

So Lewis thought until one fateful night in 1931 he took a long evening stroll with J. R. R. Tolkien, a committed Roman Catholic who had befriended Lewis some five years earlier. Tolkien shook the foundations of Lewis's fashionable skepticism by suggesting to him that the reason Christ sounded like a myth was because he was the myth that became fact. Shortly thereafter, Lewis would accept Christ as the historical savior of the world, but without thereby robbing him of his mythic power to speak to the heart as well as the mind, the imagination as well as the reason.

Lewis was thoroughly changed by his new faith, and the dozens of books that flowed from his pen over the next three decades all attest, directly or indirectly, to his belief in the Trinity, the Incarnation, the Atonement, and the Resurrection. Among his many books, all of which are still in print, are an allegorical and spiritual autobiographies (*The Pilgrim's Regress* and *Surprised by Joy*, respectively), three seminal works of Christian apologetics (*The Problem of Pain*; *Miracles*; *Mere Christianity*), two imaginative works that are utterly original in form and genre (*The Screwtape Letters*; *The Great Divorce*), a devotional book, an analysis of love, and a critique of modern education (*Reflections on the Psalms*; *The Four Loves*; *The Abolition of Man*), a trilogy of science-fictions novels (*Out of the Silent Planet*; *Perelandra*; *That Hideous Strength*), the seven Chronicles of Narnia, and a haunting Christian novel set in a pre-Christian world (*Till We Have Faces*).

Lewis further manifested his Christian commitment in a number of unique ways. First, he agreed to give a series of Broadcast Talks on the Christian religion over the BBC during the dark days of the Second World War when German planes bombarded London from the air. These talks, later collected as *Mere Christianity*, were not well received by his colleagues who thought they were too popular and, in any case, were unrelated to Lewis's specialties as a professor of literature. Second, he agreed to be the President of the Oxford Socratic Club, a group that sponsored open air debates on the truth and relevance of Christianity in the modern world. Third, he spent countless hours answering letters from fans, so much so that he dreaded the sound of the mailman. Fourth, he anonymously donated most of his royalties to charity. Fifth, he co-founded with Tolkien a Christian writers group (the Inklings) that helped inspire some of the finest Christian writing of the twentieth century.

In addition to all this, Lewis proved to be one of Oxford's finest tutors and lecturers, authoring a number of academic works that are still highly respected today, among them, *A Preface to Paradise Lost*, *The Allegory of Love*, *The Discarded Image*, and *English Literature in the Sixteenth Century Excluding Drama*. Nevertheless, despite Lewis's well-deserved fame, his openness about his faith and his decision to write popular works outside of his field prevented him from winning a professorship at Oxford. Thankfully, this oversight was remedied in 1954, when Magdalene College, Cambridge, awarded him the Chair of Medieval and Renaissance Literature, a chair specifically designed for Lewis and which he held until his death.

Though Lewis remained a bachelor well into his fifties, he ended up embarking on one of the strangest courtships in history. The woman who would become the wife of the great Oxford don was a divorced-atheist-Marxist Jew from the Bronx who, partly through reading Lewis's works, became a Christian. In 1956, to help secure British citizenship for her and her boys, Lewis married Helen Joy Davidman in a civil ceremony, never intending to live with her as man and wife. In 1957, when she contracted cancer, Lewis realized he was deeply in love with her and married her in the hospital. Miraculously, Joy's cancer went into remission, and the couple spent three happy years together.

When the cancer returned and claimed Joy's life, Lewis was devastated. As a way of dealing with his grief, he kept a journal, which was published in 1961 (anonymously at first) under the title *A Grief Observed*. Few such memoirs have dealt so honestly and nakedly with grief. Because Lewis avoided the temptation of "cleaning up" the early, despairing parts of *A Grief Observed* before publishing it, the book succeeds in chronicling a faith that is at first torn and mangled by grief but which eventually matures into a deeper and stronger faith in God's love and providence.

Ever a humble man who avoided celebrity status, Lewis would likely have been pleased by the fact that his death on November 22, 1963, received little notice, overshadowed as it was by the assassination of John F. Kennedy.

C. S. LEWIS: A TIMELINE

1895	Birth of Warren Lewis
Nov 29, 1898	Birth of Clive Staples Lewis
1908	Death of Lewis's mother
1914-1916	Studies under Kirkpatrick
1917-1918	First World War service
1925	Becomes fellow of Magdalen College, Oxford
1929-30	Converts to Theism
1931	Converts to Christianity
1933	*The Pilgrim's Regress*
1933	Lewis and Tolkien form the Inklings
1936	*The Allegory of Love*
1938	*Out of the Silent Planet*
1940	*The Problem of Pain*
1941-1944	Broadcast talks; later collected and published as *Mere Christianity*
1942-1954	President of Oxford Socratic Club
1942	*The Screwtape Letters*
1942	*A Preface to Paradise Lost*
1943	*The Abolition of Man*
1943	*Perelandra*
1945	*That Hideous Strength*
1946	*The Great Divorce*
1947	*Miracles*

Sept 8, 1947 .... Appears on cover of *Time*

1950-56 .... The Chronicles of Narnia (one per year)

1952 .... *Mere Christianity*

1954 .... *English Literature, Excluding Drama in the Sixteenth Century*

1954 .... Chair of Medieval and Renaissance Literature, University of Cambridge

1955 .... *Surprised by Joy*

1956 .... Marries Joy Davidman in civil ceremony

1956 .... *Till We Have Faces*

1957 .... Marries Joy in ecclesiastical ceremony

1958 .... *Reflections on the Psalms*

1960 .... *The Four Loves*

1960 .... Death of Joy Lewis

1961 .... *A Grief Observed*

Nov 22, 1963 .... Dies at the Kilns, aged 64

1964 .... *The Discarded Image*

A to Z
with C. S. Lewis

ASLAN

As an English professor, I have spent the last two decades guiding college students through the great books of the western intellectual tradition. And yet, though I have taught (and loved) the works of Homer, Sophocles, Virgil, Dante, Chaucer, Shakespeare, Milton, and Dickens, I do not hesitate to assert that Aslan is one of the supreme characters in all of literature. Though many readers assume that Aslan, the lion king of Narnia who dies and rises again, is an allegory for Christ, Lewis himself disagreed.

According to his creator, Aslan is not an allegory for Christ but the Christ of Narnia. The distinction is vital. Were Aslan only an allegory, a mere stand-in for the hero of the gospels, he would not engage the reader as he does. In fact, as Lewis explained, Aslan is what the Second Person of the Trinity (God the Son) might have been like had he been incarnated in a magical world of talking animals and living trees. As such, Aslan takes on a force and a reality that speaks to us through the pages of the Chronicles of Narnia.

In Aslan, we experience all the mighty paradoxes of the Incarnate Son: he is powerful yet gentle, filled with righteous anger yet rich with compassion; he inspires awe and even terror (for he is not a tame lion), yet he is as beautiful as he is good; The modern world has ripped apart the Old and New Testament, leaving us with two seemingly irreconcilable deities: an angry, wrathful Yahweh who cannot be approached, and a meek and mild Jesus who is too timid to defend his followers from evil. Aslan allows us to reintegrate—not just intellectually and theologically, but emotionally and viscerally as well—the two sides of the Triune God who calls out to us on every page of the Bible, from Genesis to Revelation.

Every time a character comes into the presence of Aslan, he learns, to his great surprise, that something can be both terrible and beautiful, that it can provoke, simultaneously, feelings of fear and of joy. Borrowing a word from Rudolf Otto, Lewis referred to this dual feeling as the numinous. The numinous is what Isaiah and John felt when they were carried, trembling and awe-struck, into the throne room of God, and heard the four-faced cherubim cry out "holy, holy, holy!" It is what Moses felt as he stood before the Burning Bush, or Jacob when he wrestled all night with God, or Job when Jehovah spoke to him from the whirlwind, or David when he was convicted of his sin with Bathsheba and experienced (all at once) the wrathful judgment and infinite mercy of the Holy One of Israel.

Our age has lost its sense of the numinous, for it has lost its sense of the sacred. Through the character of Aslan, Lewis not only instructs us in the nature of the numinous, but trains us how to react when we are in its presence. When we finish the Chronicles, we may not be able to define the numinous, but we know we have felt it: each and every time Aslan appears on the page.

BEAUTY

Those who have not had the opportunity to study literature at a college or university may be surprised to know that most English departments in our nation (secular and sacred) have thrown out the concept of beauty. If that statement does not shock you, then consider a doctor who cares nothing about health, or a philosopher who cares nothing about wisdom, or a scientist who cares nothing about the laws of nature. What would you think about such people? You would think they were frauds who had betrayed their profession and were running their race in vain. And you would be right!

For the last three millennia, beauty has been the end, the goal, and the criterion of great literature (not to mention music, dance, and the visual arts). Men wrote poetry as a way of approaching that divine Beauty which transcends the ceaseless change and decay of our world. They yearned for a kind of balance and harmony that was not subjected to death and corruption, that celebrated wholeness and clarity, that dwelled together with goodness and truth, and that carried in its wake understanding and illumination.

Lewis is best known as an apologist for the Christian faith, but he was also an apologist for beauty. With great courage, he resisted those who sought to deconstruct beauty and convert it from an essential element of the Creation inscribed by God in the heart of man and nature into a bourgeois construct, a tool of the status quo used to enforce conformity. Rather than give in to the modern Cult of the Ugly, which embraces ugliness as a form of freedom and self-expression, Lewis championed the pursuit of beauty as an affirmation that we were created in the image of a God who is Himself the standard of Beauty, Truth, and Goodness.

Lewis dramatizes this titanic struggle between essential Beauty and the Cult of the Ugly in part three of his Space Trilogy, *That Hideous Strength*. In the novel, which fuses domestic drama with apocalyptic fantasy, Lewis introduces us to N.I.C.E. (the National Institute of Co-ordinated Experiments), an anti-Christian, anti-beauty, anti-humanistic society that worships the decapitated head of a criminal that they have managed to preserve through their occult science.

Near the end of the novel, Lewis's male hero (Mark Studdock) prepares to be initiated into the inner circle of N.I.C.E. To induce him to reject Christ and accept the Head, Mark is thrown into a lop-sided room whose function is to disrupt all standards of beauty and thus pervert his natural human reactions. What Mark is confronted with in the room is an illusion of order that continually deconstructs itself. Every time he tries to rest his eyes or mind in one corner of the room, his attempts are frustrated. The point of the exercise—which disturbingly mimics what thousands of undergrads have faced in literature classes across America—is to get Mark to reject Beauty, Form, and Meaning, and embrace, in its stead, the void.

But the exercise backfires! By being confronted with ugliness in all its horror, Mark is pressed to embrace something deep within him, something he calls the Normal.

It is my prayer, as it was Lewis's, that the nihilism of the modern university will push its charges, not toward the abandonment of standards but toward a realization that standards do exist and that their source lies outside our ever-shifting world.

COURAGE

Christian theology makes a vital distinction between special and general revelation. Special revelation refers to those moments when God has communicated directly with the creatures he made. For Christians these moments include the inspiring of the Old and New Testament, the giving of the Ten Commandments to Moses, the various theophanies when God manifested his presence on earth (the burning bush, Jacob's ladder, the one "like a son of God" who stood beside Meshach, Shadrach, and Abednego, etc.), and, supremely, in the incarnation of Christ.

General revelation, in contrast, refers to those moments in which God has made his presence known in less direct ways. God displays his glory and power through nature, shows his compassion by providing rain for the harvest, writes his moral and ethical laws upon our conscience, and speaks (dimly) of the need for sacrifice and atonement in the highest myths and rituals of the pagan nations.

And in one other way. Though the full Christian virtues of faith, hope, and love were not revealed until the coming of Christ and the New Testament, the more enlightened pagans of Greece and Rome—most notably, Plato, Aristotle, Cicero, and Virgil—were able to grasp, through God's general revelation, what Christians call the classical (or cardinal) virtues: wisdom (or prudence), temperance, justice, and courage.

In Book III of *Mere Christianity*, Lewis devotes a chapter to the cardinal virtues, and most of what he says in that chapter is derived as much from the Bible as from Aristotle's *Nicomachean Ethics*. Though Christianity makes it clear that we are all sinners and that we cannot earn our salvation by righteous works, the fact remains that those who lack special revelation from God are nevertheless capable of practicing real virtues. Of the four, courage is perhaps the most vital and essential, for, as Lewis explains in *Mere Christianity*, you cannot practice the other three virtues successfully if you do not possess courage.

In *The Screwtape Letters* (#29), Lewis theorizes that one of the reasons that God created a dangerous world is to force the humans he made to make moral decisions. And to make a moral decision very often means to choose between courage and cowardice. Courage, writes Lewis, "is not simply one of the virtues, but the form of every virtue at the testing point ... A chastity or honesty or mercy which yields to danger will be chaste or honest or merciful only on conditions. Pilate was merciful till it became risky."

In our modern age, we tend to identify courage with soldiers who stand firm on the battlefield when the bullets are flying over their heads. But it takes just as much courage to stand firm against the myriad temptations we encounter in our everyday lives. To remain chaste in the face of the sexualized media blitz with which we are daily assaulted takes courage. To remain honest when it would be so easy to plagiarize a paper or change a few numbers on a balance sheet takes courage. To remain merciful in a society where most social and political issues have become polarized takes courage.

If the virtuous pagans of ancient Greece and Rome could practice the cardinal virtue of courage in a world that lacked the gospel, then it is not asking much for Christians to do the same!

DESIRE

When the Apostle Paul brought the good news to Athens, he was initially dismayed by the great number of idols that dotted the landscape of the Athenian marketplace. That is, until he noticed one idol dedicated to an unknown god. Convinced that he had found a bridge by which to connect the longings of Greek paganism with the gospel of Christ, Paul requested an audience with the Stoic and Epicurean philosophers of the city.

Having assembled the intelligentsia of Athens, Paul began by complimenting them for their religiousness, even choosing to use the word "temple" rather than "idol" to describe their myriad centers of worship. Among these temples, Paul explained, he was excited to find one dedicated to an unknown God: excited because he (Paul) had come to Athens for the very purpose of proclaiming to them the true name of that nameless God.

From one man, Paul told them, God had made all the races of men and assigned them their times and places. And he did this, not so that the nations would go astray, but "so that they would seek him and perhaps reach out for him and find him, though he is not far from any one of us" (Acts 17:27).

Augustine perhaps had this verse in mind when he began his *Confessions* with the profound observation that God made us for himself and that our hearts are restless until they rest in Him. Behind these two insights lies a firm conviction that when God created us, he implanted within us a desire for him. True, the Fall

27

has corrupted our desires, even as it has corrupted our reason, emotions, and will, but the desire that God breathed into us in the beginning remains.

It is no exaggeration to say that all of Lewis's fiction and non-fiction is underwritten by our ineradicable longing for God. The reason Lewis was able to build so many bridges of faith to so many diverse people may have less to do with the power of his logic than with the wide appeal of his apologetics of desire. Without denying original sin, Lewis called on his readers to search within themselves for that deep yearning that cannot be denied or effaced.

In his finest sermon, "The Weight of Glory," Lewis explains that our desire for God and our desire for heaven are, ultimately, the same desire. And because they are the same, Lewis feels confident in asserting that no one who truly desires heaven will miss it. For to desire heaven is not to desire some mercenary reward, but to long for reality itself—to long to dwell for eternity in the direct presence of the One who made us for Himself.

Too often, Americans fear that their desires are too strong, and that they must therefore deny them if they are to achieve salvation. In sharp contrast to this semi-gnostic view of the body and its longings, Lewis assures us that the real problem with our desires is not that they are too strong for heaven but that they are too weak.

"We are half-hearted creatures," writes Lewis, "fooling about with drink and sex and ambition when infinite joy is offered us, like an ignorant child who wants to go on making mud pies in a slum because he cannot imagine what is meant by the offer of a holiday at the sea. We are far too easily pleased." Heaven promises a purification, not a mortification, of our deepest desires.

EASTER

Most readers of *The Lion, the Witch and the Wardrobe* have no trouble seeing the parallels between Aslan's death on the Stone Table and the Crucifixion of Jesus Christ. In both cases, the innocent Aslan and the sinless Christ are killed on behalf of a traitor (Edmund, Adam and his heirs) whose betrayal and disobedience have enslaved them to the power of the enemy (the White Witch, the devil). For Lewis, in both cases as well, the blood shed by the righteous scapegoat provided the ransom to buy back the traitor from the power of evil.

In Narnia, this exchange is called the deeper magic—an ancient promise that when an innocent, willing victim died in the place of a traitor, the Stone Table would crack and death would start working backwards. In our world, the exchange is called the atonement—the powerful and eternal promise that when Christ died on the Cross, he brought us back into a right relationship with God the Father.

As a pledge of those promises, both Aslan and Christ rose from the dead, and, in doing so, crushed the power of the White Witch and the devil. In Narnia, this resurrection occurs at dawn, some six hours or so after Aslan is killed; in our world, it occurred on the third day, on that first glorious Easter morning.

That Lewis means these two resurrections to parallel one another is also something that few readers miss. However, there is a deeper level to Lewis's reworking of Easter that often goes unnoticed by even the most careful reader—a reworking that has the power to open our eyes to a dimension of the Resurrection that is too often overlooked by Christians.

In Lewis's telling, after Aslan rises from the dead, he leaps into the courtyard of the White Witch's castle to rescue the poor Narnians whom the Witch has turned to stone. One by one, Aslan goes up to the statues and breathes on them, causing them to regain their status as living creatures. Though Lewis does not say this directly, it is implied that before experiencing and defeating death, Aslan did not have the power to breathe on statues and bring them back to life.

In 1 Corinthians 15, Paul makes a vital distinction between the first Adam, whom God made a living soul, and the last Adam (Christ), whom God made a life-giving spirit. Unlike Adam (that is, us), who possessed a life that eventually ran down and died, the Risen Christ possesses Life itself—a life that can never get sick or grow old or die.

In *Mere Christianity* (IV.1), Lewis makes an equally vital distinction between our own mortal, creaturely life (*bios* in Greek) and the eternal, indestructible Life of God (*zoe*). To become a Christian does not mean gaining more *bios:* to do so would merely extend our life by a few decades. No, becoming a Christian means having our *bios* killed and replaced with *zoe*.

And that is why, Lewis concludes, the transformation from an unregenerate sinner to a saved saint is less like a sick man becoming a healthy man and more like a statue coming to life.

When Christ rose again on that first Easter Sunday, he went *through* death (*bios*) and came out on the other side. As a result he now possesses Life (*zoe*) and can share that Life with others.

FAITH

The childish notion that faith means "believing in something you know isn't true," is, alas, still very much with us. That faith might mean what Hebrews 11:1 says it means ("confidence in what we hope for" and "assurance about what we do not see") seems counter-intuitive and even foolish to a modern age that insists on founding all its beliefs on empirical evidence. "If I can't see it or hear it or touch it or taste it or smell it," so the saying goes, "it doesn't exist."

Even amongst believers, Christianity is too often thought of as an emotional "leap of faith" that lays aside reason and logic in its search for spirituality. Faith, it is often argued, is meritorious in itself, apart from its object. Belief makes us strong, despite the content of that belief.

Although Lewis was well aware that no one can reason himself into the Kingdom of God and that there comes a point of surrender to super-natural realities that transcend all human logic, he was convinced that the acceptance of Christ could be a reasoned step of faith, rather than an existential leap. Christianity, Lewis demonstrates in his books and essays, makes sense: it embodies a worldview that is logically consistent and squares with the world around us.

Christianity says we were made in God's image but fell into sin. Does not the fact that we all possess the innate ability for great good and great evil—that we each have a little Mother Theresa and a little Hitler within us—make this teaching both rational and self-evident? Christianity says Christ was the incarnate Son of God, 100% human and 100% divine. That may sound irrational, yet are we not ourselves incarnational beings (fully physical and fully spiritual), and does not marriage and sexuality represent an incarnational mingling of the two into one?

The Bible says Christ turned water into wine and fed 5000 men with five loaves and two fish. But every day, water turns into wine, a little grain blossoms into much grain, and a few fish multiply into many. It says as well that Christ died and rose again. But then there is not a single oak tree in the forest that did not spring from a dry, lifeless acorn that was buried in the ground.

The great miracles and doctrines of the Christian faith are written deep into our world and our psyche, if only we have eyes to see and ears to hear. Yes, we are told, seeing is believing, but it is just as often the case that believing is seeing.

So the faith that draws us to Christ need not be irrational or illogical, but what of the faith that sustains us in Christ? Too often, writes Lewis in an essay titled "Obstinacy in Belief," the modern world expects Christians to continually question their faith. That may sound reasonable on the surface, but it does not hold up to scrutiny.

What would you think of a man who married a woman and then immediately began to spy on her every time she left the house? You would think the man was a fool and a lout, for he refuses to put faith in the love he shares with his wife and the vow that cemented their marriage. And yet that is exactly what the modern world expects Christians to do: to question the God they have vowed to serve every time something goes wrong or an incident occurs that cannot be explained. Christians put their faith not in a temporal idea but an eternal Person. To doubt that Person after surrendering our life to him would reveal us to be not only faithless but foolhardy.

GREAT DIVORCE

Though I have a deep love for all the works of C. S. Lewis, if I were forced to choose just one book, it would have to be *The Great Divorce*. And yet, though this richly imaginative book draws together all that is most unique and insightful in Lewis's thought, there are many who have not read it because they are dissuaded by the strange title. "Why should I read a book about divorce?" they reason with themselves, "and, in any case, what is so great about divorce!"

To understand Lewis's title, we must first understand another book with an even stranger title: *The Marriage of Heaven and Hell*. Written—or, to be more accurate, engraved—by the British Romantic poet and artist William Blake in 1790, *The Marriage of Heaven and Hell* propounds a thesis that is more postmodern than modern: that heaven and hell are merely states of mind.

Midway through his work, Blake has a devil take an angel on a tour of hell. With language and imagery reminiscent of Dante and Milton, Blake presents a horrific picture of hell replete with giant spiders and burning sulfur. However, the moment that the angel leaves, hell transforms from an inferno of despair and pain to a "pleasant bank beside a river by moonlight."

Though there are many parts of Blake's *Marriage* that are hard (if not impossible) to decipher, his meaning in this passage is quite clear: hell only appears dreadful to those who have adopted an absolute view of morality that makes a sharp division between devils and angels, hell and heaven, darkness and light. In direct contrast to this Judeo-Christian view of good and evil, Blake asserts that what the Bible calls sin represents not disobedience but a failure in perception.

"If the doors of perception were cleansed," promises Blake, "every thing would appear to man as it is, infinite. For man has closed himself up, till he sees all things thro' narrow chinks of his cavern." According to Blake, salvation comes not through confessing one's sin and accepting the forgiveness of Christ, but by learning to see the world differently. Neither heaven nor hell has any absolute reality—all is determined by the way we choose to perceive it.

The "great divorce" Lewis announces in his book not only shatters Blake's moral and theological relativism but asserts a truth about heaven and hell that Blake refused to acknowledge. What if, Lewis's book wonders, the damned were allowed to ride a bus from hell to heaven? And what if, when they got there, they were met by the souls of the blessed who tried to convince them, even now, to give up their sin and pride and embrace the mercy of Christ? What would they do?

In all but one instance, the sinners freely choose to return to hell. Their rejection of grace has not only blinded them to the truth; it has robbed them of their humanity. They are, to borrow a phrase from *The Last Battle*, so afraid of being taken in by the saints sent to help them that they cannot be taken out of their self-imposed imprisonment and willful exile from God.

Surprisingly, Lewis agrees in part with Blake. "Hell is a state of mind ... And every state of mind, left to itself, every shutting up of the creature within the dungeon of its own mind—is, in the end, Hell. But Heaven is not a state of mind. Heaven is reality itself." Heaven and hell cannot be married: one might as well try to unite life and death, growth and decay, love and narcissism, substance and shadow, truth and error, that which is and that which is not.

HEAVEN

Why, Lewis asks in *Miracles*, do we always speak of God and heaven in negative terms? We are corporeal, we say, while God is non-corporeal. Earth is physical; heaven is non-physical.

The truth, as presented in Scripture, is quite different. The God of the Bible is not non-corporeal but trans-corporeal. He is *more* than the creatures he made, not less. We are personal, conscious beings, not because we were created by an impersonal, unconscious force but because the One who made us is both trans-personal and supra-conscious.

In the same way, heaven is not non-physical but trans-physical. God's dwelling place is *more* than, not less than, our own. Heaven is not earth with all the "stuff" taken out, but ultimate reality. Though Plato was wrong to speak of our world as an illusion, as an insubstantial imitation of an imitation, Lewis was right to suggest (in the final chapter of *The Last Battle*) that *compared to* the thundering reality of heaven, our earth is but a shadow-land.

Our misunderstanding of heaven rests in part on our misunderstanding of our own human nature. We are not, as Plato thought, souls trapped within bodies but enfleshed souls: not half body and half soul, but 100% physical and 100% spiritual. And when we die, that duality will persist.

Though I love the film *It's a Wonderful Life*, I'm afraid it has led many Christians astray. Let me state it clearly: we do *not* become angels when we die. Angels are fully spiritual beings, even as animals are fully physical. But we, the great amphibians of the universe, were created to be enfleshed souls and will remain so in heaven.

Even so, Jesus Christ, who assumed our nature in the Incarnation—becoming fully God and fully man—will remain incarnate for eternity. Rather than return to heaven as pure spirit (as the First and Third Persons of the Trinity are pure spirit), Christ rose in a Resurrection Body with which he will be clothed forever.

When the last trump sounds and the old earth and old heaven pass away, we too shall be clothed in Resurrection Bodies and live upon a new earth that is *more*, not less, physical than our present planet. Indeed, in *The Problem of Pain*, Lewis suggests that there will be animals in heaven—not because Lewis thought animals had souls, but because he could not believe that heaven would be robbed of the physical glory of the lion, the bear, and the elephant.

In *The Great Divorce*, Lewis imagines what might happen if the souls of the damned were allowed to board a bus in hell and ride on it to heaven. In keeping with Lewis's firmly biblical view of a trans-physical heaven, when the shrunken souls of the damned (Lewis compares them to greasy stains on a window pane) step off the bus, they find that the grass of heaven is so physical, so substantial that they are unable to bend it. In fact, in a bravura display of heavenly irony, Lewis depicts the damned as being able to walk on the water—not because they are Christ-like, but because the water is too solid to allow their ghostly bodies to penetrate it.

Yes, our world is real, but its temporal reality offers us but a glimpse, a faint foreshadowing of the greater reality that is to come.

INFLUENCE

C. S. Lewis was the greatest Christian apologist of the twentieth century. But he defended far more than Christ and the Bible. In addition to championing the Christian worldview, he was an advocate for that period of history when all of Europe embraced the faith: the Middle Ages.

Rather than accept 200 years of Enlightenment propaganda that had dismissed the Middle Ages as a time of darkness, ignorance, and superstition, Lewis called on his readers to take a second look at the medieval period. In his fiction, his non-fiction, and his academic books and essays, Lewis consistently presented the Middle Ages as a positive era in which society was galvanized by a unified vision of God, man, and the universe.

In one of those academic books, *The Discarded Image*, Lewis even took the time to lay out the medieval model of the universe. Whereas our age views the universe merely as our house, the Medievals considered it their home. They often referred to it by its Greek name (cosmos), for the word cosmos connotes something about the heavens that is absent from the Latin "universe."

Cosmos shares the same Greek root as cosmetics: a root that means "ornament." Just as cosmetics are used to ornament the face of a woman, so the Medievals viewed the cosmos as the ornament of God. It showed forth God's glory, beauty, and splendor, even as man himself does.

As God is ordered and harmonious so is his cosmos. The Medieval who looked up at the night sky, Lewis explains, reveled in the intricate balance of the heavens, which he believed stretched above him in a series of perfect concentric circles. Each of the seven "planets" (Moon, Mercury, Venus, Sun, Mars, Jupiter, and Saturn) was fixed in a crystalline sphere, and as the planets spun in their eternal orbits, they produced a celestial music known as the music of the spheres. Alas, though that heavenly melody plays all around us, our ears have grown too dull to hear it.

And as each planet turned in its sphere, it cast down a heavenly influence that produced metals in the earth and imprinted a personality type upon those born beneath its cosmic revolutions. Thus, while the moon produced silver and inspired lunacy, and Venus produced copper and made men amorous, Mars drew iron out of the ground and inspired a martial spirit in those on whom it shed its influence. (In his fine book, *Planet Narnia*, Michael Ward argues, convincingly, that the seven Chronicles of Narnia are patterned, in part, after the influences of the seven planets.)

Though such a notion may seem absurd to citizens of the modern world, we must not forget that most people today believe that a microscopic strand of information known as DNA determines everything about our life and character. Now it is true that there were some superstitious Medievals (as there still are some today) who believed that the stars controlled their fates, but that was not the official view. For most believers, it was, and is, up to us to receive the influence properly.

A woman born under Venus could be a passionate wife or a reckless harlot; a man born under Mars could be a knight or a warlord. Even so, the same sun that makes clay hard and brittle makes wax soft and pliable. Though Lewis did not advocate a simple return to the medieval notion of influence, he encouraged his readers to take seriously their interactions with the cosmos and to choose wisely how they used the gifts and personalities that were given to them.

JESUS

No person has ever had a greater impact on the history of the world, and yet no person has been the focal point of more controversy and strife. No person has ever been worshipped with such devotion or manipulated with such selfish ingenuity. For well over a century, an ever-changing band of biblical "scholars" (some of them genuine, but most of them self-appointed) have organized themselves under the rubric of the Jesus Seminar and have taken as their goal the grail-like search for the "historical Jesus."

Sadly, though the majority of their findings are based on their readings of Matthew, Mark, Luke, and John (with an occasional gnostic gospel thrown in), most members of the Jesus Seminar refuse to treat the canonical gospels with the respect they deserve. And that despite the growing number of historians and textual critics who have judged the gospels to be reliable historical documents based on eyewitness accounts that corroborate, rather than duplicate, one another.

Though C. S. Lewis was not a trained biblical scholar, he *was* an expert reader of literature with a fine eye for the distinctions between genres. Long before modern scholarship confirmed the historical accuracy of the gospels, Lewis had already explained to his readers that the Jesus of the gospels and the "historical Jesus" of revisionist scholarship were one and the same.

Anyone who reads the gospels alongside other ancient texts will immediately see the difference. There is nothing legendary about the gospels. They are, Lewis asserts, sober biographies grounded in real, down-to-earth details—the kind of details that do not appear in literature until the nineteenth century. As for Jesus himself, he emerges from the gospels with a concrete reality that surpasses all other figures in the ancient world (only Socrates comes close). When we read the gospels, we *know* Jesus in a way we do not know anyone else before the modern period.

As for the claims Jesus makes in the gospels, Lewis, in what is perhaps his best known apologetical argument, defuses all those critics who would treat Jesus as a good teacher or prophet and nothing more. In *Mere Christianity* (II.3), Lewis gives the lie to this attempt to domesticate and defang the historical Jesus of the gospels.

Again and again, Lewis reminds us, Jesus makes incredible claims about himself: he is the Way, the Truth and the Life; he is the Resurrection and the Life; he is one with the Father; he has the authority to forgive sins; he calls on people to follow him (and not just his teachings); he takes upon himself the power to reinterpret the Law.

A person who made these claims and was not the Son of God would not be a prophet or even a good man. He would either be a deceiver on a grand scale or a certifiable maniac. Yet the overwhelming consensus of the gospels and of those who knew Jesus rule out the possibility that he was either a liar or a lunatic. Once these two options are eliminated, however, we are left with only one possibility: that he was who he claimed to be.

And that is why Lewis concludes that we can shut Jesus up as a lunatic, kill him as a devil, or fall at his feet in worship—but "let us not come with any patronizing nonsense about His being a great human teacher. He has not left that open to us. He did not intend to."

KINGSHIP

America is a country that does not like kings! We threw off George III in the late eighteenth century and have (with the exception of FDR) limited our presidents to two terms in office.

And yet, most Americans harbor a fascination with the throne and the crown. We love to follow the ins and outs of the British royal family, we flock to fantasy films that feature strong and courageous kings, and we patronize renaissance festivals that recreate a world run by noble lords and ladies clad in magnificent clothing and possessed of genteel manners.

Though most Americans grow up with an almost innate distrust of class distinctions (our Constitution actually forbids the granting of hereditary titles), we devour *The Lord of the Rings* and The Chronicles of Narnia—books that rejoice in medieval hierarchy and pageantry. The reason for this, I would suggest, is that the Creator implanted in us a yearning to honor and serve something greater than ourselves. And though that yearning will not be fully consummated until we stand before the throne of Christ the King, I believe that something deep within us longs for the glory and splendor that surrounds true earthly kingship

Though Lewis understood that democracy was, practically speaking, the most successful form of government and allowed for the most individual freedom, he knew that a desire for kingship was written in the collective heart of the human race. Not, of course, for tyrannical monarchs who rob their people of their wealth, their liberty, and their dignity, but for true God-appointed kings who rule with truth, justice, and honor.

Near the end of *The Voyage of the Dawn Treader*, Lewis explains to us what true kingship means when King Caspian announces that he will abandon his ship, forsake his crown, and sail on to the end of the world in search of adventure. Though Reepicheep the mouse is a loyal subject of the Narnian throne, he makes it clear to Caspian that he cannot do what he wishes: "'You are the King of Narnia. You break faith with all of your subjects …if you do not return. You shall not please yourself with adventures as if you were a private person.'"

Though the king has power and authority, he is not to use it to please himself but to bring order and stability to his realm. The king is not a private person but belongs to his people. Indeed, when Shasta/Cor (in *The Horse and His Boy*) says he would rather not be king, he is quickly informed that the "'King's under the law, for it's the law makes him a king. Hast no more power to start away from thy crown than any sentry from his post.'"

As for the true subjects of the king, they understand that the presence of a rightful monarch assures them of their dignity rather than robbing them of it. That is why when (in *Prince Caspian*) the evil dwarf Nikabrik says he has had enough of human kings, Trufflehunter the Badger first identifies himself proudly as a beast and then speaks up boldly for proper order and hierarchy: "'This is the true King of Narnia we've got here: a true King coming back to true Narnia. And we beasts remember, even if Dwarfs forget, that Narnia was never right except when a Son of Adam was King.'"

Hierarchy, properly understood, gives purpose, meaning, and integrity to king and subject alike.

LOVE

Christians are fond of declaring that "God is love," and we are right to do so (1 John 4:16). But what do we mean when we say God is love? How could God have been love in that timeless time that preceded his creation of us and our world? Before God spoke the universe into being, there was nothing to love, so how can we say that God is love?

In answer to this question, Lewis reminds us (*Mere Christianity* IV.4) that the Christian God is not radically singular (as he is in Islam) but exists as an eternal Trinity: Father, Son, and Holy Spirit. God is not some lonely, radically monotheistic deity, but three Persons in one God. He is, if it is not too absurd to express it thus, his own community.

When the Bible declares that God is love, it does not mean that he is the Platonic Form of love (Love with a capital "L") or that he is love in some abstract, idealistic sense. It means that he is love in action. For all eternity, the Father has loved the Son and the Son has loved the Father, and the love between them is so real, so substantial that it is itself a Person: the Holy Spirit.

We've all been part of group or club in which the spirit between the members was so strong that it was almost a felt presence. Well, in our world, that spirit of camaraderie is only that— an almost tangible feeling of unity between the members—but within the Godhead, it is a living Spirit that shares equally in the deity of Father and Son.

Actually, love is ultimately not a feeling at all, but an action, a dynamic activity. In Christianity, to be truly and fully saved means not just to have our sins washed away and to spend eternity in heaven. It means nothing less than participating in the triune life and love of God.

Even on the earth, love manifests itself in its fullest form as a movement out of the self toward the other person. True marriage, Lewis writes, is not founded on a feeling ("being in love") but on an active love that draws husband to wife and wife to husband.

Many of the divorces in our country are caused by the wrongheaded notion that the only true foundation of marriage is the feeling of being in love. Unfortunately, once this premise is accepted, it means that the moment one spouse ceases to feel warm feelings toward the other, he or she is free, if not obligated, to end the marriage.

Now it is true that the feeling of love *does* strengthen a marriage, but that love proceeds out of the *action* of love (the movement out of the self toward the other), and not vice versa. Indeed, Lewis advises husbands who no longer feel love for their wives to start treating them *as if* they loved them. If they do that for several weeks, Lewis assures them, the feeling of love will return.

In the same way, when the Bible commands us to love our enemies, it does not mean that we are to feel warm emotions toward them. Of course we don't feel warm emotions toward them! But, if we will treat them in a loving manner, we will often find that we are capable of feeling positive emotions toward them as well. This is even more true of charitable acts toward the poor. The more we treat the less fortunate with acts of compassion, the more we will find a capacity within us to feel true (rather than hypocritical and self-righteous) emotions of pity and love.

MYTH

Although most readers of C. S. Lewis know that he spent much of his life as an atheist, few realize that Lewis's journey to faith did not take him directly from atheism to Christianity. On the contrary, Lewis spent over a year as a theist (a believer in God but not in Christ) before he was able to accept the Trinity, Incarnation, Atonement, and Resurrection.

What held Lewis the theist back from embracing Christianity was his great knowledge and love of mythology. From his passionate study of Sir James Frazer's *The Golden Bough*, Lewis knew that every ancient culture was aware of the pervasive power of human sin and guilt, particularly as it manifested itself in terms of forbidden acts or taboos. In order to deal with such taboos, these cultures not only practiced rituals of sacrifice and ablution, but harbored a cherished myth about a god who came to earth, died, and then returned to the abode of the gods.

Frazer referred to this divine, or sometimes semi-divine, scapegoat as the Corn King, for his death and rebirth paralleled the seasonal cycle of the grain: what Americans call wheat, the British call corn. As the grain is harvested and milled but then returns to life in the spring, so the Corn King is killed and buried, only to be reborn and renewed.

In Greece, the Corn King goes by the name of Adonis or Bacchus. In Egypt he is called Osiris. Amongst the Babylonians and Persians, he bears the name of Tammuz and Mithras. And in the northern regions of Scandinavia, he is called Balder.

Given the persistence of the Corn King across all ancient cultures, Lewis concluded (along with most of his fellow academics) that Jesus of Nazareth was nothing more than the Hebrew version of the Corn King myth. That is, until one fateful night when he took a long walk with his friend J. R. R. Tolkien (author of *The Lord of the Rings* and a committed Roman Catholic). As they strolled along Addison's Walk on the grounds of Magdalen College, Oxford, Tolkien suggested something to Lewis that revolutionized his understanding of myth and the Christian gospel.

What if, Tolkien suggested, the reason Christ sounded so much like the Corn King myth was that Christ was the myth that became fact? To put it another way, perhaps the reason that every ancient culture yearned for a god to come to earth, to die, and to rise again was because the Creator who made all the nations placed in every person a desire for this very thing.

And, if that is the case, then does it not make sense that when God enacted his salvation in the world, he did it in a way that fulfilled the desire that he put in all of us? Indeed, if the life, death, and resurrection of Christ had been a wholly foreign thing, with no glimpses or foreshadowings in the myths and legends of the world's peoples, then it would seem that Christ was an alien god, one whose plan of salvation bore no resemblance to our most ancient and persistent longings.

But if Christ is the fulfillment of all the legends of the Corn King—if he is truly the myth that became fact—then the God of the Bible is not just the God of the Jews but of all the nations. Christians believe that the events of Good Friday and Easter Sunday fulfilled the messianic prophecies recorded in the Old Testament. What Lewis learned from Tolkien is that Christ fulfilled as well all the deepest yearnings of the pagan peoples.

NICENESS

If you ever watch a movie in which a non-Christian actor plays a Christian character, you will often notice that he will convey his character's faith by means of a friendly, if oafish-looking, grin. Though it is possible that unbelieving actors do this to parody believers, I would suggest that the real reason is rooted in a characteristically American misunderstanding of the nature of that glorious new life that Christ promises his followers.

There exists in our country a widespread belief that Christians are—or at least should be—"nice" people who spend most of their day smiling. Though it is, in most cases, a good thing to smile, to be thankful, and to takes things lightly, niceness is hardly the central virtue of the Christian faith. Christ's goal is to transform us into saints, not improve our personalities.

In *Mere Christianity*, Lewis argues that the reason God tells us not to judge is that we do not know the raw material that other people are struggling with. The world expects all Christians to act equally happy and outgoing, but the fact is that it may be a greater victory for Christian A (who has been strapped with a weight of inner demons and psychological complexes) to smile than for Christian B (who has been blessed from birth with a loving family, a healthy body, and sound finances) to donate $5000 to charity.

As a patriotic American of conservative convictions, I am no fan of the young men who avoided the draft in the 1970s by running off to Canada, but I consciously avoid casting judgment upon them. The reason for this is simple. Since I was born too late to have been eligible for the draft, I have no way of knowing how I would have reacted in their place. To take a more difficult case, I cannot in good conscience judge the Germans who remained silent during the holocaust. Of course I would like to believe that, if I had been in their place, I would have risked imprisonment to shelter fugitive Jews in my attic. But how do I know if I would have had the courage to do so?

The point of this exercise is not to turn morality into something that is relative to the times; sin and cowardice are the same in any age or culture. The point is that none of us can ever really know the struggles that go on within the hearts and minds of our fellow human beings.

And that takes us back to niceness. The reason it is wrong for the world (and the church) to make a smiling face and a friendly demeanor the defining mark of the Christian is that the Body of Christ is made up of people whose personality types are as diverse and unique as the wavy lines of a fingerprint. If every Christian in America were the smiling, friendly type, then that would mean that God only loves (and saves) smiling, friendly people.

In fact, God is no respecter of persons, and his church is therefore filled with people who are grumpy, cantankerous, depressed, irritable, and painfully shy. Two of the greatest heroes of Narnia are the crotchety, suspicious Trumpkin and the perpetually gloomy, infuriatingly pessimistic Puddleglum. Yet from their seemingly intractable raw material, Aslan molds two of the bravest and most loyal warriors in the realm.

The power of Christ lies not in his ability to make us nice, but in his capacity for transforming our hurt, our pain, and even our sin into tools and weapons for bringing his kingdoms to earth.

OBEDIENCE

There are very few citizens of the western world who do not know the story of the Garden of Eden. Even those who have never picked up a Bible or seen the inside of a church are aware that a great deal of trouble was caused when two people named Adam and Eve ate an apple they were not supposed to eat. Unfortunately, many who know the story think of it only in magical terms: a cursed fruit is plucked and eaten and a sinister enchantment brings suffering into the world.

In fact, as Lewis argues in at least three of his works (*The Problem of Pain*, *A Preface to Paradise Lost*, and *Perelandra*), the apple in and of itself was not that important. The vital part of the story is that in tasting of the apple the first man and woman disobeyed the direct command of their creator. It was their disobedience, not some dark magic locked up in the fruit, that caused us to Fall from our original state of perfection.

God, writes Lewis the English professor, intended for us to be adjectives, but we, in our rebelliousness and pride, insisted on being nouns. We were made to modify God, not to stand on our own in lonely defiance; to give him glory and honor, not to steal it for ourselves.

Before the Fall, our entire being was oriented toward obedience to God. As long as our soul obeyed God, our body obeyed our soul. Indeed, Lewis theorizes that pre-fallen Adam could (like certain modern gurus in Tibet) control his autonomic functions by sheer willpower. Better yet, as long as we remained in a state of innocence, our obedience to God came naturally, almost effortlessly. True, it did call for an act of will, but our yielding to God was as easy and pleasant as the yielding that lovers make to each other on their honeymoon.

Sadly, after the Fall, our obedience to God became a hard and bitter thing. No longer easy and pleasant, the choice to surrender our will to God now strikes all of us (young and old, male and female alike) as a kind of little death. At times, we all succumb to what Lewis, in *The Problem of Pain*, calls "the black, Satanic wish to kill or die rather than give in."

Yet still God calls us to obey him, not for his good, but for ours. For we cannot fulfill our purpose as creatures when we are in rebellion against our creator. That is why the devil will do all that he can to provoke and enflame in us a spirit of disobedience.

In *The Screwtape Letters* (#8), a senior devil warns his nephew of the dangers of obedience. At all costs, humans must be prodded to forsake the will of God (whom Screwtape calls the Enemy) and insist on choosing their own path and making their own decisions free from divine control.

To drive home his point, Screwtape creates a scenario which fills him with dread and horror: "Our cause is never more in danger than when a human, no longer desiring, but still intending, to do our Enemy's will, looks round upon a universe from which every trace of Him seems to have vanished, and asks why he has been forsaken, and still obeys."

There can be no greater victory in the Christian life than this: to obey God when we are confused and frightened and in despair. To obey God, not because we want to, but because God is worthy of our obedience. To obey, and, by obeying, trust and love, the God who made us in his image.

PAIN

God, Christians declare, is all-powerful and all-loving. And yet, the pain and suffering in our world suggests that God is either too weak to eliminate it or too apathetic to care to do so. That, in a nutshell, is the problem of pain, and it is has stood for centuries as one of the crowning arguments against the existence of the God of the Bible. Skeptics from Hume to Richard Dawkins have offered the problem of pain as incontestable proof that our universe is *not* run by a benevolent personal God who works miracles and involves himself in human history.

As an apologist, Lewis knew that he could not hope to challenge the skeptics of his own day if he did not make some attempt to address this problem in his writing. Accordingly, Lewis's first full-fledged apologetic work was not *Mere Christianity* or *Miracles*, but *The Problem of Pain*.

In Chapters 2 and 3 of that book, Lewis argues that pain is the upshot of God's free-will experiment. In asserting the existence and necessity of human free will, Lewis does not mean to imply that we are free to do anything we want or that God is not sovereign. Rather, he reminds us that as creatures made in God's image, we possess consciousness, rationality, and will. God did not intend to create a race of puppets, but of moral beings who think and choose and create.

Though the vast majority of Christians would agree with Lewis on this point, few take the time to draw out the implications of God's choosing to give us a will distinct from his own. God cannot give us choice and take it away in the same breath; that would be a contradiction, and God, Lewis boldly asserts, does not violate the law of non-contradiction.

If God truly meant for us to be moral agents, Lewis theorizes, then he would have to create a playing field where we could act out our choices. However, to ensure that we could not manipulate that playing field to suit our own whims (and thus impinge unfairly upon the choices of other moral agents), he would have to make the field both fixed and stable. Unfortunately, for the field to be fixed and stable, God would have to leave open the possibility that his creatures would collide with it, causing discomfort and even pain.

Our world, Lewis suggests, may not be the best of all possible worlds, but it may be the only possible *kind* of world God could have created to allow us to engage in His free-will experiment. Of course, a critic will be quick to point out that God could turn rocks into pillows every time one of us fell down, so that we would not bruise our head. Well, Lewis admits, God *does* sometimes do just that when he performs a miracle, but if God were to change nature every time someone was in danger of being hurt, the game, as a game, would not be playable.

So the fixed nature of our world—necessary if we are to enact our free will—makes pain an ever-present possibility. But that is only part of the story. Too often Christians, especially American Christians, believe that God created us to have a good time. But that was never his intent. He created us to grow into something greater, even if that process of growth involves pain and suffering. Yes, Lewis concludes, God may at times treat us harshly, but he has never treated us with contempt. To the contrary, he pays us the "intolerable compliment" of loving us fully and irrevocably. And that love demands that we grow into the creatures he created us to be, no matter the cost. It is the beloved son, not the servant, whom the father disciplines.

QUEST

In the western world, the most famous quest is that for the Holy Grail. But every nation, every culture, every religion has its great quest story. Something deep within our psyche compels us to go on pilgrimage, to leave our home and take to the road. The inner call that sends us forth promises to provide us with adventure and mystery but with something else as well—something less tangible. At the end of the quest lies the promise of meaning, purpose, fulfillment.

The Greeks used the beautiful word "telos" to refer to that purposeful end that we spend our lives in search of, but in English we have a similar word that rivals the Greek in its beauty and power. At various stages in our lives, we who speak the tongue of Shakespeare and Milton seek after a consummation (from two Latin roots that mean "all together").

Like "telos," consummation connotes the achievement of a final goal or end, whether in business, in art, or in life itself: the "consummation devoutly to be wished" that Hamlet seeks in his "To be or not to be speech" is death. But it is also used to refer to that physical and spiritual moment when a new husband and wife join themselves sexually and become one flesh. To find consummation is to achieve a happiness that is really a kind of completion. In the moment of consummation, we know who we are, why we are here, and how we fit in to the greater plan.

In *The Voyage of the Dawn Treader*, Lewis reprises a character he created in *Prince Caspian*: Reepicheep, king of the talking mice. Whereas Reepicheep plays the role of a simple, if chivalrous knight in *Prince Caspian*, in *The Voyage of the Dawn Treader*, he develops into something grander and more wonderful. If he is a little like Lancelot (the bravest of the knights) in the former tale, then he is a great deal like Galahad (the finder of the Grail) in the latter. Still fearless and a bit reckless, Galahad-Reepicheep turns his talents and energy toward a magnificent, never-before-attempted quest: to set his foot upon the shore of Aslan's Country.

Since Aslan's Country is heaven, Reepicheep's quest can only end with that consummation that we call death. But that does not dissuade the courageous mouse from taking up the challenge. He will sail east, to the place where the sun rises, and he will not stop until he has found the true home of the Risen Lion King of Narnia.

What will he do, what will he risk, what will he sacrifice to achieve that goal? Reepicheep himself gives the answer: "'My own plans are made. While I can, I sail east in the *Dawn Treader*. When she fails me, I paddle east in my coracle. When she sinks, I shall swim east with my four paws. And when I can swim no longer, if I have not reached Aslan's country, or shot over the edge of the world in some vast cataract, I shall sink with my nose to the sunrise and Peepiceek will be head of the talking mice in Narnia.'"

When my kids were younger, they spent many hours watching the Disney Channel. At first, I was pleased to see how many characters in the shows they watched spoke with passion about following their dream. That is, until I realized that all their talk about following their dream had little to do with consummation: it was mostly about being a pop star. Thankfully, children who read Reepicheep's story will learn of a greater dream: one that calls for true courage and sacrifice; one that will reveal to us, in the end, the very purpose for which we were born.

REASON

John Paul II's papal encyclical "On the Relationship between Faith and Reason" (*Fides et Ratio*) is an important work that should be read by all thinking Roman Catholics and Protestants who care about the life of the mind. And yet, though I am a great proponent of the encyclical, I feel a great sadness that it had to be written in the first place!

In the centuries before the Enlightenment seized control of our wisest and best educated scholars, no one would have been surprised to see the words "faith" and "reason" placed side by side. After all, Christianity invented the university, and the Christian worldview shaped some of the finest minds in history: Augustine, Dante, Aquinas, Luther, and Pascal, to name but a few. Likewise, the scientific achievements of such men as Roger Bacon, Copernicus, Galileo, Francis Bacon, Kepler, and Newton were all underwritten by their faith in a super-natural Creator.

Had C. S. Lewis grown up in the medieval or renaissance periods, his training in logic and rhetoric would have been carried out in direct conversation with the doctrines of Christianity. As a citizen of the modern world, he was trained instead by an atheistic tutor named Kirkpatrick who used reason to inoculate Lewis's mind against religious "superstitions."

But life has its little ironies. When Lewis became a Christian, he did not forget Kirkpatrick's teachings. Rather than throw the baby out with the bathwater, Lewis marshaled the full weight of logic and reason to defend the faith from its modern detractors. With great boldness, Lewis restored a great truth that had been forgotten: namely, that reason is on the side of the angels.

In *Miracles*, for example, Lewis argues that naturalism (the belief that nature is all that there is and that nothing super-natural exists) is self-refuting. If we are merely products of evolutionary forces guided (or "un-guided") by time and chance, then we have no reason to trust our senses or our powers of logic to arrive at the truth. In fact, if naturalism is true, then truth itself becomes impossible—for truth stands outside nature, but the naturalist says nothing stands outside nature.

The modern naturalist too often overlooks the fact that the laws of naturalism rest on abstract principles that lie outside the supposedly closed system of nature. To formulate such principles we must step outside the flow of nature to achieve a perspective that is, quite literally, super-natural. But if naturalism is true, then we cannot do that. If the naturalists are right and nature is a vast, impersonal, unguided mechanism, then how can we have any knowledge of that mechanism? Surely an objective judge who is not pre-committed to a naturalistic worldview would conclude that our knowledge and understanding *of* nature cannot be a *part* of nature.

So Lewis explains it in *Miracles*, but it is in *The Screwtape Letters* that he drives the message home with a bracing wit that is not soon forgotten. Again and again, senior devil Screwtape advises his nephew to do whatever he can to *prevent* his patient from engaging his reason.

The job of the devil is not to make us think but to fuddle our minds—to keep us endlessly fixed on the daily stream of life. God, in contrast, would fix our attention on things we cannot see, on laws and theorems and principles that transcend the stream. It was God, Screwtape concedes, who created reason and logic; against it, the devils can only offer propaganda, jargon, and spin.

THE SEXES

Young people are taught many damaging things in our great secular universities. From Marxism to Freudianism, moral relativism to postmodern deconstruction, their heads are filled with insidious, anti-humanistic theories that, when carried out to their logical conclusion, cause chaos, confusion, and despair on both the social and personal level.

And yet, I would argue that the most damaging thing they are taught slips under the radar of most attentive parents. In thousands of sociology and psychology classrooms across our nation, students are taught that there is no such thing as masculinity and femininity. That our sexual natures are not innate and God-given. That the only reason boys and girls are different is that we give boys trucks to play with and girls dolls to play with.

Though any free-thinking, open-minded parent who has raised a boy and a girl knows that this is patent nonsense—that boys and girls manifest their inborn, hard-wired masculinity and femininity from a very early age—this absurd and poisonous theory of the sexes is taught as gospel truth throughout the western world. Indeed, as a way of advancing their false view of the sexes, feminists insisted on doing away altogether with the word "sexes."

Rather than speak, as people have spoken for centuries, about the male and female sex, they have forced academia and the media to speak of the male and female gender. They don't like the word "sex" because it connotes an essential link between the masculine/feminine body and the masculine/feminine soul—and that is a reality they are desperate to obscure. Gender carries with it no such connotation. Gender is not something we were created with but a social construct that is reinforced by cultural mores and behavioral expectations.

As a Christian who not only believed the clear and simple teachings of the Bible (namely, that God *created* us male and female) but who possessed an intimate understanding of human nature, C. S. Lewis never succumbed to the feminist attack on masculinity and femininity. He knew and celebrated the essential differences between the sexes: a celebration that is beautifully expressed in *Prince Caspian*. Narnia, held captive by the "post-Christian" Telmarines, cannot be rescued and renewed until Peter and Edmund exercise their masculine gifts to defeat the Telmarine army while Susan and Lucy exercise their feminine gifts to wake up the trees from their deep slumber.

However, Lewis's crowning statement of the distinct but complementary natures of masculinity and femininity comes in *Perelandra*. Near the end of the novel, Lewis allows us to gaze on the angelic guardians of Perelandra (Venus) and Malacandra (Mars). In keeping with the ancient association of Venus with the female principle and Mars with the male, Lewis discovers in them a masculinity and femininity that reaches deeper than society or biology or language can fathom.

Although the two angels are not physically male and female, they embody the essence of masculinity and femininity. Thus, whereas Malacandra has "the look of one standing armed, at the ramparts of his own remote archaic world, in ceaseless vigilance," Perelandra's eyes open "inward, as if they were the curtained gateway to a world of waves and murmurings and wandering airs." For Lewis, both forms of seeing are necessary; together, they bring wholeness.

TAO

Mere Christianity is Lewis's best known and most complete work of apologetics. In it he begins with a general argument for theism (the existence of God) and then expands that argument into a specific defense of the Christian gospel. From there, he goes on to explain and support the central moral and theological principles of Christianity.

Although Lewis believed firmly in the authority of scripture, he knew that many of his modern readers did not share his belief. Accordingly, Lewis carefully builds his apologetical arguments on common ground: on facts and observations about our world and ourselves that all people, regardless of their religious beliefs, can see, understand, and acknowledge.

That is why he begins *Mere Christianity* with an unexpected statement that seems, on the surface, to have little to do with a defense of the Christian faith. Did you ever notice, Lewis writes, that when two people disagree about something, they argue about it rather than fight? Though most of us likely did not notice this phenomenon before, the moment we read Lewis's statement, the truth of it becomes apparent. Of course we argue instead of fight!

And that's when Lewis hooks us. Whether we realize it or not, two people cannot argue about something unless they agree (often unconsciously) to a fixed standard that transcends them both. When we argue, we take that standard for granted and then make a case (sometimes rationally, sometimes irrationally) that our side of the argument better approximates that standard.

In a case where two former business partners are suing each other for fraud, neither party says: "yes, I swindled my partner, and I was right to do so." If he did, he would not be sent to jail; he would be sent to an asylum. Now, one party might partially confess to fraud, but then he would follow the confession by offering mitigating circumstances to show that the "fraud" was actually justified. In other words, he still holds to the accepted standard that fraud is wrong.

On the basis of our shared experience of such ethical debates, Lewis posits that a universal, cross-cultural moral code exists and is binding. In *The Abolition of Man*, he gives that law code a name: the Tao. Many Christians are confused by this: why should Lewis borrow a word from Taoism (a classical school of Chinese thought) to bolster his case for the Christian faith? The answer is simple: to show that *all* people (east and west) recognize the Tao, even though they continually break it.

Many relativists will balk against Lewis's assertion of the Tao, claiming that morality veers wildly from culture to culture and is a man-made (rather than a divinely-given) thing that alters from age to age. But those same so-called relativists will quickly change their tune if someone robs them. "It was wrong of you to do that," they will say, and if the person who robbed them says, "in my culture it is OK for me to steal," the relativist will not accept the excuse.

The fact is everyone knows the Tao exists, for whatever our own personal ideology, we expect other people to treat us in accordance with the Tao. Indeed, if there were no Tao, then no court could have tried the Nazis or Saddam Hussein or the perpetrators of apartheid. The Tao *does* exist, but if it exists, then it makes necessary a director of the Tao who transcends all times and cultures. It requires, in short, a super-natural Creator who inscribed the Tao into our conscience.

UNIVERSALISM

Near the end of *The Last Battle*, a noble Calormene soldier named Emeth dies and comes before Aslan, the Christ of Narnia. Although Emeth hails from a distant land that worships a false god named Tash (rather than the true Aslan), and although Emeth has served Tash all his life, when he meets Aslan, he is welcomed by the Great Lion and invited into heaven.

Of all the passages in the voluminous writings of C. S. Lewis, none has caused more controversy and confusion than this suggestion by the orthodox Christian Lewis that salvation can be attained outside of Christ. Indeed, when I speak about Lewis, the most common question that I am asked is whether or not the episode with Emeth reveals Lewis to be a Universalist in disguise: that is, someone who believes that all who practice their religion faithfully—whether they be Christians or Jews, Muslims or Hindus—will be saved.

It does not. Had Emeth come before Aslan and requested directions to the Tash part of heaven, and had Aslan obliged, then Lewis would be a Universalist. But that is not what happens in the episode. Quite to the contrary, when Emeth stands before Aslan, he realizes and accepts that Tash is false and Aslan true, and that the deep spiritual desire he has followed all his life has found its fulfillment in Aslan. He proves this by falling to his knees in worship.

Like the Magi of the Christmas story, he recognizes that Aslan (not Tash) is the end of his journey. In response, Aslan assures him: "'unless thy desire had been for me thou wouldst not have sought so long and so truly. For all find what they truly seek.'"

Now, it must be admitted that though this is not universalism, it does border on a concept that the vast majority of believers would reject (rightly) as unbiblical: post-mortem ("after death") salvation. Orthodox Christian teaching states that all decisions for or against Christ must be made before we die. Once we pass to the other side, all bets are off. Though many Protestants think that the Catholic belief in purgatory allows for a second chance at salvation, it does not. In Catholicism, those who reach purgatory are already saved; they just need to be sanctified.

So is Lewis an advocate of post-mortem salvation? This time I must be a bit more nuanced with my answer. Yes, Emeth is technically dead when he accepts Aslan's offer of salvation, but that does not mean he is being given a "second chance."

As Lewis explains in a number of his works, God lives in eternity, not in time. Too often, people think that eternity means time going on forever, when what it really means is that time itself does not exist. The closest we come to a perception of eternity, Lewis writes, is our experience of the present moment. For the present is the point where time touches eternity.

The moment Emeth dies is an eternal moment—and that eternal moment contains all the other moments of his life. He accepts Aslan (Christ) in that eternal moment, because all of the other moments have been building up to that acceptance. And once he does, all the other moments become reoriented around that moment of decision. That is why, in *The Great Divorce*, Lewis says heaven and hell work backwards. For those who accept Christ in that eternal moment, it will seem, not that they have just entered heaven, but that they have always been there.

VIRTUE

It is a sad thing that our modern world has redefined virtue in negative terms. Rather than define a virtuous man as someone who actively practices the positive virtues of prudence, courage, justice, and temperance, we turn things on their head and celebrate the goodness of those who don't succumb to folly, don't betray an excessive amount of cowardice, don't violate anyone's rights, and don't drink or smoke.

Such is the case with the four classical virtues, but it is even more so with the three theological ones. We celebrate those who stay true to the course, who press on, who don't give up, not those who have put their faith in an unseen Creator and their hope in his promises. Even when we do praise faith and hope, it is generally a vague, non-creedal faith in humanity or fate or the universe and a hazy, content-less hope in, well, something or other.

As for love, Lewis was fond of critiquing his age for replacing the positive love (*caritas, agape*) of the Bible with a negative form of unselfishness. Although the highest pagans (Aristotle) and the great Christian ethicists (Aquinas) taught that virtue is a habit gained by practicing virtuous actions, we of a more "enlightened" age have embraced a distinctly "hands off" ethos.

Rather than actively love our neighbor, we unselfishly allow him to live whatever way he wants to, even if his life choices are self-destructive. Had Lewis lived today, I think he would have said that the reigning virtue is not unselfishness but tolerance—a pseudo-virtue that also manifests itself, not in active charity, but in a negative acquiescence to the "rights" of others.

In *The Screwtape Letters* (#26), junior tempter Wormwood is counseled by his more experienced uncle to teach his human patient "to surrender benefits not that others may be happy in having them but that he may be unselfish in forgoing them." Though this strategy of replacing love with unselfishness may look the same on the outside, it has a very different effect on the soul of the one surrendering the benefits. Far from moving out of himself toward the other (which is what love calls us to do), the practitioner of the negative virtue of unselfishness uses the other person as a way of bolstering his own sense of piety and self-righteousness.

Actually, if truth be told, love and unselfishness are also *received* in a radically different way by the object of the proffered charity. In the former case, the recipient is assured that another human being cares deeply about him; in the latter, he feels manipulated and used.

G. K. Chesterton once defined a humanitarian as someone who loves humanity but hates human beings. The person who is on the receiving end of unselfishness knows instinctively, to paraphrase a line from Letter 26, that he is being treated as a sort of lay figure upon which the would-be humanitarian exercises his petty, self-centered altruisms.

When the virtues are enacted in a positive, healthy spirit, they draw us closer to God and our neighbor. But when they are turned back upon themselves as a method for bolstering our ego and self esteem, they ensnare and isolate us. The false humanitarian ends up feeling contempt for his fellow man because he cannot move outside his own desperate need to feel good about himself. But the virtuous man who practices true love comes to truly love the people he serves.

WAR

The eighteen-year-old C. S. Lewis was hardly what one would call an athletic young man. He was a failure at sports and spent his school days avoiding the company of upper-class athletes. And yet, in 1917, the bookish Lewis chose to enlist in the First World War. I say chose because Lewis, as an Irish citizen (he grew up in Belfast), was not subjected to the draft. Nevertheless, he served and fought in the trenches, returning to England a year later as a wounded veteran.

Though he was too old to fight in the Second World War, he supported the war effort in every way he could, including speaking over the BBC radio and giving live talks to the RAF. In 1940, he even addressed a pacifist society in Oxford on the reasons why he (Lewis) was not a pacifist (his speech is anthologized in *The Weight of Glory and Other Addresses*).

In his talk, Lewis respectfully reminds his audience that when Christ instructed his followers to turn the other cheek, he likely meant the command to refer to personal situations between people and their neighbors. There is no indication that the command was meant to apply to all situations at all times. Surely, Lewis argues, "turn the other cheek" does not forbid me from coming to the rescue of someone who is being chased down by a maniac with a knife!

Christ calls upon us not to harbor a spirit of self-righteous hatred and retaliation toward those who have injured us. But that does not mean that magistrates, parents, teachers, and soldiers should suffer themselves to be struck by citizens, children, students, or enemy combatants.

Besides, Christ himself showered his greatest praise upon a Roman military officer (Luke 7:9). Likewise, when John the Baptist was approached by soldiers in search of spiritual advice, he did *not* tell them to quit their jobs—he merely told them not to extort money or accuse people falsely (Luke 3:14). Both Peter (1 Peter 2:14) and Paul (Romans 13:4) called upon the early church to obey magistrates, who do not bear the sword in vain.

In *Mere Christianity* (III.7), Lewis makes some of the same arguments, though this time he calls on his readers to examine their own hearts carefully. All killing, Lewis insists, is not murder: a proper translation of the Ten Commandments would read "Thou shalt not murder," *not* "Thou shalt not kill." Still, if we ourselves hear about the death of enemy soldiers or the execution of a criminal and rejoice in the loss of life, then we have fallen outside the high call of Christ.

"We may kill if necessary," writes Lewis, "but we must not hate and enjoy hating. We may punish if necessary, but we must not enjoy it. In other words, something inside us, the feeling of resentment, the feeling that wants to get one's own back, must be simply killed."

Yes, Lewis knew and felt that war was a dreadful thing. No one who fought in the killing fields of the First World War could doubt that. Still, Lewis believed that if we could remove the hatred and resentment from our soul, if we could free ourselves from brooding on revenge, that war could be approached courageously with "a kind of gaiety and wholeheartedness."

Lewis was no fan of war, but he was unashamed to champion the beauty of the knight, of the medieval Crusader, of the "Christian in arms for the defense of a good cause."

X-RAY

Of all the books that Lewis wrote, the most difficult and obscure must surely be *The Pilgrim's Regress*. In this strange, esoteric allegory of his journey to faith, Lewis introduces us to an everyman character named John who grows up in the legalistic, pharisaical land of Puritania, where everyone wears masks and the people are burdened by laws they cannot follow.

One day, however, John catches a glimpse of a distant island populated by bearded enchanters in a deep state of meditation. The vision provokes in John a sweet desire for goodness, truth, and beauty, and he sets off on a pilgrimage to find the source of that desire. Sadly, in seeking out the source of his joy, John continually takes wrong turns and falls off the true path.

As in John Bunyan's *Pilgrim's Progress*, each of the temptations that John faces along the way is allegorized as a person or place. The difference between Bunyan and Lewis's versions of the road to faith—and the thing that makes the former infinitely easier to comprehend than the latter—is that whereas Bunyan's pilgrim faces such spiritual traps as sloth, despair, and vanity, Lewis's pilgrim faces a score of intellectual dead ends (stoicism, idealism, materialism, aestheticism, scientism, and so forth) that lie outside the experience of the average reader. Indeed, what makes Lewis's work particularly challenging is that many of the "isms" he critiques have been abandoned, even by the secular humanists who once championed them.

Generally speaking, John faces two types of dangers—a cold rationalism (identified with the north) that kills joy and desire, and a hot hedonism (identified with the south) that causes joy to sicken and desire to grow perverse. In his journeys through the north, John is taken into custody by Sigismund Enlightenment, who, in the manner of Sigmund Freud, tries to convince him that his desire for the island is an illusion, an adolescent form of wish fulfillment.

John is then thrown into a dungeon where he must face a giant whose eyes pierce through him like a merciless X-ray machine. The giant's eyes, writes Lewis, "had this property, that whatever they looked on became transparent. Consequently, when John looked round in to the dungeon, he retreated from his fellow prisoners in terror, for the place seemed to be thronged with demons. A woman was seated near him, but he did not know it was a woman, because, through the face, he saw the skull, and through that the brains and the passage of the nose."

Lewis shows great insight in comparing the giant to an X-ray, for the enlightenment theories of Freud, Marx, and Darwin have had just that effect on modern man. Though the writings of these founding fathers of modernism vary widely, they are alike in being, at their core, reductive. By reducing human love, joy, religion, and art to a product of unconscious urges, or economic forces, or the struggle for survival and reproduction, the theories of Freud, Marx, and Darwin have emptied humanity of its freedom, its dignity, and its purpose.

Meditating on the destructive force of the Enlightenment X-ray, Lewis closes his book, *The Abolition of Man*, with these prophetic words: "You cannot go on 'explaining away' for ever: you will find that you have explained explanation itself away. ... If you see through everything, then everything is transparent. But a wholly transparent world is an invisible world. To see through all things is the same as not to see."

YOUTH

C. S. Lewis dedicated the first of his Narnian fairy tales, *The Lion, the Witch and the Wardrobe*, to Lucy Barfield, the daughter of his good friend, Owen. In the dedication he offers this sage advice: "My dear Lucy, I wrote this story for you, but when I began it I had not realized that girls grow quicker than books. As a result you are probably already too old for fairy tales, and by the time it is printed and bound you will be older still. But some day you will be old enough to start reading fairy tales again."

Near the end of *That Hideous Strength* (a novel to which Lewis added the wonderful subtitle, "A Modern Fairy-Tale for Grown-Ups"), the male hero, Mark Studdock, comes within inches of selling his soul to a demon-run secret society with plans to take over the world. As part of the initiation rite, he is thrown into a lop-sided room which is intended to destroy within him any last vestige of his belief in goodness, truth, and beauty.

Mark almost gives in, but then a still small voice within him rises up and asserts the existence of something normal and right and whole, of which the lop-sided room represents the perversion. Saved by that sudden illumination, Mark runs for his life. In his flight, he hides out in a small country hotel, where he rests for a moment in a quiet sitting room. In the room, Mark notices two shelves filled with bound copies of a periodical known as *The Strand*.

"In one of these he found a serial children's story which he had begun to read as a child but abandoned because his tenth birthday came when he was half way through it and he was ashamed to read it after that. Now, he chased it from volume to volume till he had finished it. It was good. The grown-up stories to which, after his tenth birthday, he had turned instead of it, now seemed to him, except for *Sherlock Holmes,* to be rubbish."

Most modern academics who read the above paragraph would criticize, if not ridicule, Lewis for his "puerile sentimentality." They would, of course, be wrong to do so. Lewis was unique in the academia of his day for championing (along with his good friend, J. R. R. Tolkien) children's literature and fantasy novels as serious genres deserving serious consideration.

Rather than dismiss youthful innocence and joy as immature emotions to be cast off on the road to adulthood, Lewis treasured (as did Jesus!) that child-like view of the world that opens itself to faith and hope and that can discern magic and wonder in even the most mundane of things.

Lewis found nothing wise or mature or even realistic in the cynicism and skepticism of his academic colleagues. Indeed, because he was not too proud to look for them there, Lewis discovered great insights in *Aesop's Fables, The Wind in the Willows, The Tales of Beatrix Potter, Alice in Wonderland,* and the children's stories of George MacDonald and E. Nesbitt.

In fact, though it is not well known, we have Lewis and Tolkien to thank for the post-1950's resurgence of children's literature and fairy tales. Both genres, which were strong and healthy during the late Victorian Age, had fallen out of favor in the first half of the 20th century. The success of The Chronicles of Narnia, *The Hobbit,* and *The Lord of the Rings* helped restore the reputation of these discredited genres, thus enabling moderns to draw on their innocent wisdom.

ZEITGEIST

Zeitgeist is a German word that means "spirit of the age." The zeitgeist of Periclean Athens was self-knowledge (supremely embodied in the thought of Socrates), while that of the Middle Ages and Victorianism was hierarchy (Dante) and progress (Tennyson), respectively. As for the darker zeitgeist of modernism, marked by relativism and subjectivism, though Lewis did not embody it, he understood it better than many of its most ardent supporters.

In a sense, all of Lewis's books offer a critique of modernism, but the one that does so with the deepest insight and the greatest prophetic power is *The Abolition of Man*. In this brief book, which bears the rather intimidating subtitle of "Reflections on Education with Special Reference to the Teaching of English in the Upper Forms of School," Lewis predicts (with woeful accuracy) what the outcome will be for a society that trains its youth in accordance with the principles of aesthetic subjectivism and moral and ethical relativism.

At the core of the modern zeitgeist, Lewis locates a refusal to abide by any fixed, transcendent standards of the Good, the True, or the Beautiful. Everything now is subjective. The old verities are up for grabs. No longer do our beliefs point back to a divine law code or an essential, in-built sense of good and evil; they exist only and solely in the eye of the beholder.

Lewis begins his analysis of this deeply-entrenched relativistic zeitgeist by highlighting an elementary textbook that teaches children that the so-called sublimity of a waterfall does not rest in the waterfall itself but in the perceptions of the one looking at it. Though this distinction may seem unimportant, Lewis shows how such a subjective view of the power of a waterfall leads in time to a subjective view of all judgments of value.

What happened in the twentieth century is that we went from relativizing all matters of beauty and sublimity (not only in nature but in the arts as well) to relativizing all matters of right and wrong. Thus, whereas modern schools revel in scientific facts and sociological statistics, they ridicule "old fashioned" notions of courage, patriotism, and honor. And yet, ironically, at the very moment we have thrown out traditional values, and the supernatural standards on which they rest, we cry out desperately for the very duty and self-sacrifice that such values make possible.

"In a sort of ghastly simplicity," warns Lewis, "we remove the organ and demand the function. We make men without chests and expect of them virtue and enterprise. We laugh at honor and are shocked to find traitors in our midst. We castrate and bid the geldings be fruitful."

For thousands of years, parents and teachers have ensured the maintenance of civilized life by training their children and students not only to understand and obey the God-given, conscience-approving standards of right and wrong, but to nurture proper feelings vis-à-vis those standards. Thus, we teach young people to feel an inner sense of pride and self-respect when they perform a virtuous action and an inner sense of shame and disgust when they chose instead the way of vice.

The sign that our society is disintegrating is not to be found in the wildness of teenagers (that has always been with us), but in the fact that when those teens commit immoral actions, they feel neither guilt nor remorse. Such chest-less young people are the vanguard of a new Dark Age.

Film Reviews

THE WARDROBE, THE WITCH AND THE LION

"In these days of wars and rumors of wars—haven't you ever dreamed of a place where there was peace and security, where living was not a struggle but a lasting delight?" With this question, Frank Capra begins his great epic film, *Lost Horizons*. Based on the novel by James Hilton, Capra's film transports a group of displaced pilgrims from the war-torn Chinese city of Baskul to the mystical land of Shangri-la. After being kidnapped by a seemingly mad pilot and then crash landing on the snowy summit of an inaccessible mountain in Tibet, our pilgrims trudge their way up a treacherous, frozen path, turn a corner, and ... gaze down into a green and fertile valley. It is one of the most magical moments in film history.

War in England; War in Narnia

In the 2005 screen version of C. S. Lewis's *The Lion, the Witch and the Wardrobe*, director Andrew Adamson allows us to experience this same transition from a world of war and madness to a land of wonder and magic. Although Lewis tells us in Chapter I that the four Pevensie children are evacuees from London, the film allows us to witness—in realistic and even harrowing detail—both the bombing of London by Nazi planes and the difficult separation of the four children from their mother.

The world from which these children are fleeing, the film makes clear, is truly one of wars and rumors of wars, a world of struggle that offers neither peace nor security. Even the cynical viewer who would dismiss fantasy as mere "escapism" would have to admit that this is a world to escape from. The starkness of the opening scenes makes the moment when Lucy, and later her siblings, pushes her way through a musty old wardrobe into a snowy Narnian wood all the more enchanting and breathtaking. Here, surely, is a place of rest. Or is it?

Narnia, as it turns out, is going through its own version of the Second World War, with a totalitarian White Witch who would devour the freedom of Narnia and a noble Lion—a symbol for Christ but also the symbol for England—who will, like Winston Churchill, stand alone if he must against the Witch's tyranny.

It is a vital part of both novel and film that the danger of Narnia becomes apparent quite quickly; neither we nor the children are given the luxury to tiptoe through the tulips of a restored Eden. The children must fight for their Shangri-la with the same dedication and faith as their father back home is fighting for the freedom of England; a point that is latent in the book but is made much more strongly and clearly in the film through the addition of some well-written, pointed dialogue.

Narnia is as much worth fighting for as England, and the stakes are just as high. Neither the European nor the Narnian war is a mere matter of trading rights or border disputes; it is about good versus evil, freedom versus slavery, light versus darkness. In Narnia, however, those sides are more distinct, embodied not only in Aslan and the White Witch but in their individual followers.

Heroes and Traitors

As they did for The Lord of the Rings trilogy, WETA Workshop has crafted creatures that convey by their outward appearance the virtue or vice of their inner nature. It is thrilling, in a modern age that has increasingly caved in to moral relativism, to see a film that so clearly takes delight in crafting a world of moral certainty. That, of course, is not to say that either novel or film gives us simple, cardboard good guys and bad guys.

Novel and film present us with both a collaborator turned patriot (Tumnus) and a good English boy who gives in to envy and despair and turns traitor (Edmund). And the film goes one better than Lewis. Not only is the character of Tumnus skillfully fleshed out (he is the son of a dead "resistance fighter;" his decision not to turn over Lucy is partly influenced by a brief, powerful encounter he has with Aslan; he ends up in the same dungeon with Edmund but shows himself more loyal), but the film adds a second character, a quick-witted fox who works in the Narnian "underground" and dies a martyr.

In such a world, it will not do for the Pevensie children, even Lucy, to remain innocent of the opposing natures of good and evil. They must understand what is at stake, and they must take sides. They must become heroes and heroines; indeed, they must become kings and queens. (Perhaps influenced by the first Harry Potter novel/film, Adamson, unlike Lewis, has the loyal Narnians immediately begin to treat the Pevensies as though they were kings and queens from the outset.) Adamson's children—as opposed to Lewis's—are not only given more chances to display courage, but engage in a fuller dialogue, both external and internal, on the nature of heroism. One of the best bits of "added dialogue" occurs when Peter is about to fight Maugrim the wolf; chief henchman of the Witch's Gestapo-like secret police. Susan, justifiably afraid that her brother will be killed, cries out to him that just because Father Christmas gave him a sword, that does not make him a hero.

Adamson also develops further the strength that the Pevensies take from their unity as a family. He retains Professor Kirke's "liar/lunatic/lord" argument in the beginning of the film—either Lucy is crazy, lying, or telling the truth about her trip to Narnia—but has Kirke add that Peter and Susan should also trust Lucy because they are family. This focus on family trust and unity is established in the opening scene when Mrs. Pevensie makes Peter promise to protect his three younger siblings (also not in the novel). Peter stays true to this promise, and Adamson even inserts several brief episodes in which Peter tries to make his siblings return to England and safety while he remains behind to fulfill his obligations to Narnia.

All this is to say that the film's development of Peter, Susan, Edmund, and Lucy is in many ways better than the novel—though the particularly moral and theological dimensions of Edmund's temptation, sin, and betrayal are muted and even somewhat muddled. We truly experience and believe Peter's transformation into a knight as we do Susan's overcoming of her skepticism and fear and Edmund's sincere repentance and maturation into a brave and selfless warrior. We also sense more powerfully than in the novel the danger that the children are in. And yet, this well-handled development of the children, which marks, along with the excellent portrayal of the Witch and the brilliant realizations of the Narnian landscapes and characters, the film's greatest strength, is also its greatest weakness.

The Historical Aslan

For the expansion of the children's characters and roles comes at a very high price: the lessening of the character and role of Aslan. The shift in emphasis becomes immediately apparent in the dinner scene with the Beavers. Lewis provides us with two prophetic rhymes: one about Aslan ("Wrong will be right / when Aslan comes in sight," etc.), that is recited first and that is given far more prominence, and one about the children ("When Adam's flesh and Adam's bone," etc.). Adamson eliminates the first altogether and then makes it seem as if the prophecy about the children is the central and most important prophecy; the one that the Narnians have most been longing for.

In addition, most of the information that the Beavers share about Aslan is left out, including the vital fact that he is the Son of the Emperor Beyond the Sea. We are not even told that he is a lion—which eliminates Edmund's true reason for drawing a charcoal mustache on the stone lion he sees in the courtyard of the Witch's castle! The messianic hope that surrounds the return of Aslan is transferred almost completely to the children; it is as if Aslan is linked to the prophecy of the children, rather than the children being linked to the prophecy of Aslan.

But the weakness in the film's portrayal of Aslan goes far beyond the trimming down of the scene with the Beavers. It is bad enough that the audience is not properly "warmed up" for the arrival of Aslan; when Aslan does in fact arrive on the scene, he is a shadow of what he is in the novel, not to mention what he is in the hearts of all lovers of the books. The computer animation for Aslan is excellent, and the range of facial expressions, though rarely and not too effectively used, is admirable, but Aslan himself evokes little awe or reverence.

Except in the well-shot, and well-lit, scene when we see the newly-risen Lion, Aslan is just not majestic or powerful enough. Liam Neeson's voicing of Aslan also lacks the necessary depth and resonance. In neither form nor voice does Aslan overwhelm us as he should; he is not even backed up with an appropriate orchestral score that would help engrave his image in our subconscious (compared to the stirring scores that accompany the Lord of the Rings and Harry Potter films, the score for this film is an almost complete disappointment).

One of C. S. Lewis's key purposes in writing not only *The Lion, the Witch and the Wardrobe* but the Chronicles as a whole was to provide his child (and adult) readers with something that our age has lost: a sense of the numinous, of the holy, of the sacred.

Again and again in the Chronicles we are told that when the children meet Aslan, they realize for the first time that something can be *both* beautiful and terrible, both exhilarating and scary. When they first stand before the Lion, they are filled with joy, but their knees go "trembly."

Though Adamson does, thankfully, include Lewis's key observation that Aslan is not a tame lion, but he is good, he doesn't include it until Aslan is about to disappear from the screen, and he does not adequately visualize this aspect of Aslan's nature in the film. He also diminishes Aslan in another way. Though the film retains Aslan's definition of the Deeper Magic, it leaves out his explanation that the Witch's knowledge only goes back to the dawn of time, whereas his, by implication, goes back before the beginning. Likewise, though we are told that Aslan comes and goes—he is not a tame lion—we are not told that he has other countries to attend to. In the place of Lewis's eternal Lion, we are given something like the "historical Aslan."

A Tamed Lion

Most disappointing of all, the film leaves out the richly cinematic episode, directly after his resurrection, when Aslan wrestles with the girls on the grass. "It was," Lewis writes in Chapter XV, "such a romp as no one has ever had except in Narnia; and whether it was more like playing with a thunderstorm or playing with a kitten Lucy could never make up her mind." Perhaps no episode in the book better illustrates Lewis's insistence that Aslan is someone to be loved and caressed but never trifled with.

We *are* given the scene which directly follows—when the girls ride on his back to the Witch's castle—but the scene is terribly truncated and another chance to capture on film Aslan's overwhelming power is lost, My young son was particularly disappointed that the film left out the thrilling moment in the book when Aslan, with the girls still on his back, leaps in a single bound over the high wall that surrounds the locked castle. The film also allows Aslan to let out his victorious roar, but even this moment lacks force, power, and conviction.

Still, although the film's Aslan is stripped of much of his awe and radiance, he *does* do all of the things that Lewis has him do in the novel. The film works out the full "sacred drama" of Aslan, giving us both his death and resurrection and explaining well the distinction between the Deep Magic and the Deeper Magic; it even includes a clear sense that the Deep Magic (the Law) is something that both defines good and evil and that must at times be appeased by sacrifice. As for the Deeper Magic, Aslan is given a good added line when he says that the Witch did not understand the true nature of sacrifice.

The film also provides us with a single, wordless shot that will, I believe, remain indelible in the memories of those who see the film. The moment comes when Edmund has been rescued and is speaking alone with Aslan on a hill. In the posture and lighting of the scene, we sense powerfully the forgiveness that Aslan is extending to Edmund and the way in which that forgiveness is already changing Edmund from within. A similar shot that lingers in the mind is the image of Susan and Lucy curled up together on the Stone Table with the dead body of Aslan. All the grief of the moment, all the loss of hope and the longing for the loved one dead is conveyed in a few seconds of film.

Had there been more scenes like these, the fuller dimensions of Aslan that all but embrace us when we read the novels— or listen to the excellent radio play version produced by Focus on the Family—might have made their way more effectively into the film. Indeed, though Lucy *is* handled well in the film, the diminishing of Aslan means that we miss out on one of the key aspects of her character: her sensitivity to the moods of Aslan and her deep, intimate connection with the Lion. In the absence of a truly mystical Lion, we lose our sense of Lucy as a mystic.

As for the "crucifixion" scene, it is done as well as it possibly could be—though Lewis's altar-like Stone Table is turned into a platform-like stage. The filmmakers should be commended for making a scene that can be viewed by adults and children alike and that will fill both with a sense of dread and fear. The Witch's gloating speech over Aslan as she is about to kill him is particularly well staged and performed, and is made even more effective by an added touch of cinematic bravura: after she kills Aslan, the Witch's eyes seem to turn black. The same goes for the well-executed battle scenes, the last one including a remarkable detail that does not occur in the book, but which I think Lewis would have approved of: when the Witch rides into battle she is wearing Aslan's shorn mane.

Again, it must be emphasized that the film is faithful to Lewis's Narnian Gospel story, but that story has far less impact because Aslan is first denied his majestic build up in the conversation at the home of the Beavers, and then is not allowed to exude holiness or provoke awe in the scenes leading up to his death and resurrection.

Why, the viewer (and reviewer) must inevitably ask, is Aslan's character so shorn of its glory and power? One would have to be naïve not to lay the blame for this muting of the fullness of Aslan partly, if not in great part, on the filmmakers' fear of seeming to press the link between Aslan and Christ. This is surely the reason for denying Aslan his eternal nature and his status as the Son of the Emperor.

Memories of Narnia

But it may also be due to the director's memory of first reading *The Lion, the Witch and the Wardrobe* when he was a child (Adamson has stated that he wanted to capture his memory of that experience on film). Perhaps what really drew the young Adamson to the novel in the first place was the land of Narnia itself and the adventures of the four children rather than Aslan per se. Adamson certainly lavishes considerable care on Narnia and its various set pieces, and audiences of all ages should be enchanted. He also, as we have seen, does an excellent job with the four children, all of whom are also well cast and acted.

Most viewers will fall in love with Narnia, and for that Adamson, WETA, and all the producers deserve praise. But viewers will not leave the theater feeling the way Lucy does at the end of *The Voyage of the Dawn Treader* when she tells Aslan that it is not Narnia but *him* whom she truly loves.

And that leads us to a third reason for the diminishment of Aslan. Perhaps our modern age and cinema are not capable of fully conceiving and realizing a character like Aslan. Perhaps Lewis was right that we have lost our ability to perceive of something as being both beautiful and terrible, that we have lost, really lost, our sense of the sacred. "When they tried to look at Aslan's face," writes Lewis in Chapter XII, "they just caught a glimpse of the golden mane and the great, royal, solemn, overwhelming eyes; and then they found they couldn't look at him and went all trembly."

Does there lurk in this sentence a kind of real magic that our modern world, that not even the Hollywood Dream Factory, can capture or understand? If so, we had better start reading our Lewis again ... and our Bibles.

EVERYTHING YOU KNOW IS ABOUT TO CHANGE: CASPIAN'S BUMPY JOURNEY FROM NOVEL TO SCREEN

"Everything you know is about to change." These are the words that Doctor Cornelius speaks to Prince Caspian in the opening sequence of the 2008 film version of *Prince Caspian* as he bids him flee from the castle of his usurping uncle Miraz. But these words might just as well have been spoken by the makers of the film to the readers of the novel on which the film is based. For indeed, the changes that the film makes to plot, characters, and themes are extensive.

Battling for Narnia

This, of course, is not in itself a bad thing. As with the second and third installments of the Lord of the Rings film trilogy, many of the changes come in the form of added or extended battle scenes—and in *Prince Caspian*, these scenes are magnificent. Just as *The Two Towers* turns Tolkien's three-page battle of Helm's Deep into an epic struggle lasting thirty minutes, so *Prince Caspian* transforms Lewis's very brief overview of the hectic skirmish that ensues outside Aslan's How after the duel of Miraz and Peter into a richly cinematic, adrenaline-pumping battle of both brains and brawn.

85

As Miraz's hordes sweep down on Peter's army, Caspian and his cavalry race through one of the tunnels that extends outward from the How and knock out the supports. This clever and at first puzzling strategy causes the ground under the charging army to collapse into a giant sink hole. As the enemy troops plunge into the pit, they are cascaded by a volley from Susan's archery division. Seconds later, a secret passage opens under the grass, allowing Caspian's cavalry to charge out and outflank Miraz's troops. As in *The Lion, the Witch and the Wardrobe,* director Andrew Adamson is able to convey the intensity and even barbarity of the battle without recourse to blood or graphic savagery: both films are rated PG, though *Prince Caspian* is a far darker film in look and theme.

The film also adds a very lengthy episode that has no precedent in the book in which Caspian, the Pevensies, and their army mount a sneak attack on the castle of King Miraz. The filmmakers pull out all the stops in visualizing this midnight raid. Griffins fly Edmund and several other warriors over the castle and drop them on various turrets, whereupon they swiftly and silently take out the sentries. Reepicheep the mouse and two of his cohorts sneak through the bars to bring down the drawbridge.

At first, the plan goes like clockwork, but then things go awry, resulting in a desperate fight in the courtyard of the castle. In the end, the Narnians are forced to retreat, aided by a minotaur who sacrifices himself to hold up the gate through which the survivors escape. The fear, confusion, and self-sacrifice all coalesce to make this a truly memorable scene.

Just as the raid itself is added to the novel, so the reasons for its failure have no precedent in Lewis's original. First, the timing of the raid is foiled when Caspian impulsively seeks out the bedchamber of his uncle, whom he plans to kill in retribution for Miraz's murder of Caspian's father. Second, scores of Narnians die needlessly because Peter allows pride, stubbornness, and a refusal to accept that he does not have everything under control to delay fatally his call to retreat. To my mind, the darkest and most disturbing moment in the film occurs when Peter casts his eye back helplessly on a number of his men who are trapped in the courtyard when the minotaur dies and the gate comes crashing down preventing further escape.

The Pevensies on Edge

In their development of Peter's character, the screenwriters pick up on something that Lewis overlooks—what it must have been like for the Pevensies to return to England as children after having spent many years as adult rulers of Narnia. In Peter's case, it has made him edgy, impatient, and desperate to prove his valor and maturity. The first signal we are given of this in the film occurs in the railway station just before the children are carried back into Narnia. Peter is bumped by an older boy, and when the boy insists that Peter apologize, Peter flies into a rage and begins a brawl.

Peter's determination to be treated like an adult follows him into Narnia and compels him to do something he does not do in the novel: challenge the authority of Caspian. It also causes him to lose his focus on Aslan, not so much because he has lost his "faith," as because he feels certain that he can handle things on his own. It even opens him up briefly to the temptations of the White Witch. Only at the end of the film does Peter come to know himself and Aslan better and repent of his rash and ultimately immature behavior.

Peter's struggle with Caspian is itself aided by a significant change made to Caspian's character: namely, he is aged by about five years and, accordingly, given a more adult, more self-conscious need to exercise his own authority and to avenge his father. Caspian does not find his own character resolution until he stands with drawn blade over the prostrate body of Miraz and refuses to indulge his passion for revenge. Though these changes to Peter and Caspian are not faithful to the novel, they add a greater depth to the characters of these two troubled young men and a greater resonance to the film.

This resonance is also felt in some slighter changes made to the character of Susan, she whom readers of the Chronicles know will eventually forsake her attachment to Narnia and Aslan and thus lose her status as a queen. Perhaps in preparation for this inevitable abandonment, Adamson adds a brief bit of dialogue in which Lucy expresses her concern that Susan does not seem happy to have returned to Narnia, and Susan responds that she had finally gotten used to being a part of our world again. When Lucy points out that she is in Narnia now, Susan asks, with a touch of weariness in her voice, "for how long?"

In tandem with this exploration of Susan's confusion as to where she belongs, the film gives her a somewhat poignant crush on the handsome Caspian that intensifies her teenage angst. Since the Chronicles are very much about young people making life-defining choices and learning to accept the consequences of those choices, I feel safe in assuming that Lewis would have approved, at least in principle, with these changes—though he would surely have disapproved of the Susan/Caspian romance. As in the film version of *The Lion, the Witch and the Wardrobe*, *Prince Caspian* is at its best when it draws out the characters of its young heroes and helps the viewer to identify with their struggles.

Cinematic Magic

Also like *The Lion, the Witch and the Wardrobe*, it provides us with breathtaking landscapes and set pieces that linger in the mind. The art direction for Aslan's How is superb and captures perfectly the numinous power of this holy Narnian site. I'm sure Lewis would have been delighted at how Aslan's How subtly references both Greco-Roman and Judeo-Christian architecture: the entrance is clearly designed after the beehive tombs that lie just outside the walls of the great citadel of Mycenae, legendary home of Agamemnon; the interior, with its narrow corridors and "sacred" artwork, recalls the Christian catacombs outside Rome.

All the scenes filmed in Aslan's How are well-shot and well-lit, particularly the scene in which the White Witch is nearly brought back into Narnia. Though the scene with the hag, nicely transformed by the filmmakers into a harpy, and the werewolf, culminating in the calling up of the blue flame, is faithful to the novel, only in the film does the Witch actually appear. The Witch's reappearance within a block of ice, her need for a drop of human blood, her "semi-bewitching" of both Caspian and Peter, and her final defeat by Edmund are all additions that make both for compelling cinema and powerful character development.

Add to this the top-notch CGI work for Reepicheep, Trufflehunter, and an imposing river god, the greater role given to Miraz's advisors, the chilling designs for the Telmarine war masks, and two truly magical moments—when the children are drawn into Narnia and when a Narnian tree trunk corkscrews open to create a door back into our world—and you end up with a film that is, *as a film*, superior to *The Lion, the Witch and the Wardrobe*.

Still, though the script, direction, music, cinematography, editing, and art design of the second film are, to my mind, superior to the first, the second is far less faithful to the Christian underpinnings of Lewis's novel. Unlike the Lord of the Rings films, which, despite their considerable plot changes, successfully preserve Tolkien's Christian meditations on the nature of good and evil, life and death, virtue and vice, friendship and treachery, knowledge and power, *Prince Caspian*, though its changes make for good cinema, leaves untapped nearly all those aspects of the novel that make it specifically Christian and that raise it, thematically, above other novels in the same genre.

The film's failure in this area is most obvious in the emasculated Aslan that it presents to us, a failure I shall consider at the end of this review. Before doing so, however, I would like to explore three vital aspects of the novel that are given short shrift in the film. The first of these three aspects the film both deemphasizes and muddles; the second it, perhaps willfully, misunderstands; the third it throws out altogether.

A Tale of Two Dwarfs

Although the film does well to deepen the characterizations of Caspian and the Pevensies, it unfortunately does so at the expense of Nikabrik and, especially, Trumpkin. And that is a shame, as so much hangs thematically on the subtle contrast that Lewis draws between the two dwarfs. At the beginning of the novel, *neither* Trumpkin nor Nikabrik believes in Aslan. Both dwarfs consider Aslan and the stories of the four children to be mere fairytales and scoff at Caspian and Trufflehunter's belief in them. There, however, the similarities between the dwarfs end. Nikabrik has gone sour inside and closed off his heart in a way that Trumpkin has not.

Lewis develops this through a series of subtle but carefully drawn distinctions: 1) Nikabrik wants to kill Caspian the first time he sees him while Trumpkin refuses to harm a guest; 2) Nikabrik is willing to make an alliance with evil creatures to fight Miraz while Trumpkin is not; 3) Nikabrik cares only for the wellbeing of his fellow dwarfs while Trumpkin cares for all his fellow creatures; 4) Nikabrik wants to kill Cornelius when he learns that he is a half-dwarf and thus, to Nikabrik's mind, a collaborator with the Telmarines while Trumpkin refuses to blame Cornelius for his ancestry; 5) Nikabrik uses Caspian to achieve his own ends while Trumpkin serves Caspian obediently even when he disagrees with him; 6) Nikabrik refuses to dance with the fawns while Trumpkin makes a willing if clumsy attempt to join the dance.

The film does hint at some of these differences, but it does not work through them in any clear or systematic way. Because it fails to do so, it misses out on two spiritual messages that are central to the novel.

First, Lewis wants his readers to understand that although both dwarfs begin as unbelievers—as atheists, or at least secular humanists, who care only for practical matters—Trumpkin is able, when he meets the children and Aslan face-to-face, to open his heart to the truth. Trumpkin's spiritual journey, that rests on the distinctions listed above, is essentially left out of the film, and with it Lewis's hopeful message that God reaches out to all types of people—not just the smiling, hymn-singing, sweetness-and-light types.

The key moment in Trumpkin's movement toward faith is sacrificed by the plot rearrangement of the film. In the novel, Caspian does not blow Susan's horn until he is at Aslan's How and is trapped by Miraz's army. Cornelius counsels Caspian to send a messenger to Cair Paravel in case the help brought by the horn arrives there. Even though Trumpkin does not believe in the magic of the horn, he volunteers to go out of obedience to Caspian.

This obedience marks a turning point which culminates in a dynamic meeting with Aslan that frees Trumpkin from any further doubts. The film wrongly moves this meeting from the middle of the story to the end and robs it of most of its power. Lewis's unforgettable transformation of a crotchety old cynic into a chivalrous warrior of faith is lost, and with it, the promise that God desires and is able to work such transformations in his fallen creatures.

Second, by sacrificing the distinctions between Trumpkin and Nikabrik, the film fails to build up properly to the scene in which Nikabrik initiates the calling back of the White Witch. Indeed, the film, probably unconsciously, robs this scene of much of its meaning by allowing minotaurs to fight in Caspian's army. Although Churchill and Roosevelt apparently believed the old adage that "the enemy of my enemy is my friend"—hence their willingness to defeat the evils of Nazism with the help of the equal evils of Communism—those who fight on the side of Aslan do not accept that the ends justify the means. Granted, I did praise above the scene in which the minotaur holds up the gate, but this scene would have worked just as well had the filmmakers used a centaur or, better yet, supplied the minotaur with a back-story in which he repents of the evils of his race and chooses to identify himself with Aslan.

Nikabrik turns to the White Witch for aid for the same reason that the Jews foolishly sought help from their old enemy (Egypt) against their new enemies (Assyria and Babylon), though God had warned them not to (Isaiah 30:1-3; Ezekiel 29:6-7). Despite their initial, shared lack of faith in Aslan, the distinctions between Trumpkin and Nikabrik lead the former to Aslan, to goodness, and to hope and the latter to the White Witch, to wickedness, and to despair. None of this is made clear in the film.

The Post-Christian Telmarines

And there is something else that the film does not make clear, something that is even more central to the novel than the Trumpkin/Nikabrik dichotomy and that the film seems almost intentionally to conceal. On the one hand, I applaud the filmmakers for having the courage to plunge so quickly into their narrative, even though it means leaving out the childhood of Caspian which Lewis takes some pains to develop in his novel. On the other, I fault them for throwing out the baby with the bathwater—that is, for leaving out those aspects of Caspian's childhood that Lewis uses to establish the background for his tale. The Telmarines have not merely defeated the Narnians; they have driven them underground and eradicated even their memory.

When the young Prince Caspian, whose nurse has been telling him stories about the old Narnia, tells his uncle that he would like to have lived in the old days of the talking animals and living trees, of the high king Peter and his siblings, and of the lion Aslan, Miraz tells him that no such things or people ever existed in Narnia and that what he has heard are just fairy tales meant for babies. He even indulges in some "higher biblical criticism" to "prove" that there could not have been two kings at the same time and that therefore none of the stories can be accepted as historically true. He then orders the boy never to speak—or *think*—about such things again!

But Caspian continues to think and to dream and to hope. He is an old Narnian at heart and yearns for the old things with passion and with faith. Doctor Cornelius fans this passion and assures Caspian that he is not the only one of his race who believes and yearns in secret.

Narnia under Miraz represents more than a totalitarian state ruled by a despot. For Lewis, the Telmarines are an embodiment of post-Christian Europe—of a land and a people who have rejected the religious heritage on which their nation was built, who have relegated the sacred narratives of Christ/Aslan to mere myths and old wives' tales. Likewise, the old Narnians are not just rebels fighting a usurper but a persecuted remnant church desperately holding on to its faith in a risen redeemer-king.

The film *does* preserve Trufflehunter's faithful testimony that Narnia was only right when a Son of Adam was on the throne, but it leaves out his equally bold pronouncement that he believes firmly in the four children and in Aslan. When Trumpkin cynically informs Trufflehunter that no one believes in Aslan anymore, Caspian confesses that he believes and that if he hadn't believed before, he certainly believes now. Until meeting Trumpkin and Trufflehunter, he had been taught that dwarfs and talking animals were myths. But now that he has found that they are real, why should he not also believe that Aslan is real? Some of this dialogue finds its way into the film, but it is divorced from the credal aspect of Trufflehunter's confession and the apologetical aspect of Caspian's logic.

In a vital line left out of the film, Edmund compares himself and his siblings to Crusaders coming back to modern England. For Lewis, the Europe of his day was as much cut off from the glories of medieval Christendom as Narnia under Miraz is from the Golden Age of Aslan and the four kings and queens. The Telmarines, like the post-Christian leaders of Europe, would paint the old days as wholly dark, engulfed by ignorance and superstition.

And yet, both sets of leaders still secretly fear those "superstitions" and do all they can to prevent their return. There is more of Richard Dawkins, Daniel Dennett, and Sam Harris in Miraz than there is of Hitler, Mussolini, and Stalin. But one would not know that from watching the film. A few scattered lines of dialogue hint at the connection between Narnia and post-Christian Europe, but they do no more than hint, and they will be noticed only by viewers who have read the novel carefully.

The Waking of Narnia

Alas, no hints at all remain of one of the chief means by which Aslan recalls Narnia to its former "medieval" faith, hope, and joy. The film faithfully and effectively records the duel between Miraz and Peter, the killing of Miraz by his treacherous advisors, and the skirmish that follows, but it ignores completely what Aslan is doing, simultaneously, in the countryside. And this proves a loss not only to the deeper message of the novel but to the film itself.

Ever since D. W. Griffith's *Birth of a Nation* hit movie screens in 1915, one of the cinematic staples of film has been the careful orchestration of dual action through the use of cross-cutting (or parallel editing). Had the filmmakers chosen to preserve Aslan's doings alongside those of Peter and the army, it could have cut back and forth with increasing swiftness between the two actions, suggesting the need for everyone to do his part in the rebirth and redemption of Narnia and then culminating with even greater power in the meeting of Aslan and the Telmarines at the bridge of Beruna.

Yes, the film does allow Aslan to wake up the trees and the river god, but Lewis's lion king does far, far more in the novel. With Lucy and Susan on his back, and aided by Bacchus (the Greek god of wine) and his Maenads (wild girls who follow in Bacchus's train and indulge in a sort of divine madness), Aslan charges through the Narnian countryside freeing the hearts and spirits of his people from Telmarine censorship and repression, even as Peter and Caspian work to defeat the physical weapons of Miraz and his troops.

First Aslan visits a rigid prim-and-proper girls' school where Telmarine revisionist history is taught and all true imagination is squelched. The magic grape vines of Bacchus tear down the walls of the school exposing it to the healthy grass and sunshine, and Aslan takes into his train the one student who yearns within for beauty, truth, and goodness. He then rushes by a boys' school where, as it turns out, the students are the small-minded, priggish ones and their frustrated yet still hopeful teacher the one whose heart is rejuvenated and set free by Aslan.

And still Aslan sweeps on through the fields: "At every farm animals came out to join them. Sad old donkeys who had never known joy grew suddenly young again; chained dogs broke their chains; horses kicked their carts to pieces and came trotting along with them—clop-clop—kicking up the mud and whinnying." Aslan's freeing of the countryside climaxes with his miraculous healing of a sick old woman who turns out to be none other than Caspian's nurse, his original tutor before Doctor Cornelius. All has come full circle; the past is redeemed and Narnia is restored.

Aslan Tamed Again

The filmmakers do, it must be admitted, build up a fair amount of messianic eagerness. They unexpectedly include four lines about Aslan ("When he bares his teeth, / winter meets its death / And when he shakes his mane, / we shall have spring again") that they had sadly left out of *The Lion, the Witch and the Wardrobe*. They even make it clear that the battle cannot be won apart from Aslan. Nevertheless, they give Aslan very little to do.

Worse yet, the conviction of the battle scenes and the scenes dealing with the children do not carry over into the scenes with Aslan. The filmmakers seem merely to tick off Aslan's lines without fully believing or even understanding them. Though I consider Liam Neeson a very fine actor, he makes no attempt to "act" Aslan's lines; he merely "says" them quickly in an almost off-handed manner. Though Aslan is given two good roars, his words produce no sense of awe or reverence in the hearts of the viewer.

Several of the key lines from the novel are retained—every year you grow, you will find me bigger; nothing ever happens in the same way twice; no one is ever told what would have happened—but the dialogue surrounding these lines is so drastically trimmed back that the lines lose their resonance. They just fly by without "sticking," as if they are being said out of a sense of duty to the novel rather than out of a sense of joy or love or fervor for Lewis's great Lion.

Adamson allows us to see the intimacy between Aslan and Lucy, but not the subtle yet powerful way in which Aslan brings Lucy to understand the exact nature of her guilt, to confess that guilt, and to seek restitution. These moments in which Aslan gently nudges "naughty" children to own up to and understand their sinful behavior increase with each succeeding novel, and it is hoped that future films will be more faithful to these moments.

Likewise, Adamson retains the scene in which Reepicheep asks Aslan to restore his lost tail as well as Aslan's motivation for doing so: the great love that is between Reepicheep and his people, who are ready to cut off their own tails lest only Reepicheep go without one. But then he inexplicably leaves out the two sentences that Aslan utters when he sees the mice about to cut off their tails: "'Ah,' roared Aslan, 'you have conquered me. You have great hearts.'" Few moments in the Chronicles are more redolent of the overwhelming compassion of Aslan and the intimate way in which he, as the Christ of Narnia, allows himself to be moved both by our sorrows and our joys, our yearnings and our frustrations. For no good reason, the film robs us of that moment.

I hope that none of what I have here written will dissuade the reader from seeing this splendidly produced film. It should most definitely be seen by all who love the Chronicles, especially as it so powerfully develops the characters of the children and so effectively conjures Narnia, in all its beauty and pain, to cinematic life.

But the viewing of the film must send us back to the novel to be reminded of what the film leaves out: the subtle virtues or vices in our character that draw us toward or away from God's mercy and truth; the need for our own jaded, materialistic age to regain its sense of faith and wonder; and the need to set free not only our body and mind but our soul and heart as well.

Above all, the film's disappointing reduction of Aslan should impel us to a fresh encounter with Lewis's divine Lion that we might be reminded that something *can* be beautiful and terrible at the same time, that there is a kind of joy that makes one serious, and that only in the reverent fear of the Lord does true wisdom begin.

TEMPTATIONS AT SEA: THE *DAWN TREADER'S* VOYAGE TO HOLLYWOOD

The Voyage of the Dawn Treader is the most epic of the Chronicles of Narnia, but it is also the most episodic. Although Lewis gives the crew of the *Dawn Treader* a clearly defined mission—to seek out the seven lost lords of Narnia—the unraveling of that mission quickly resolves itself into a series of exciting but unrelated island adventures; rather like those that Odysseus encounters on his long journey home from Troy. It is therefore not surprising that the filmmakers who set themselves the task of adapting Lewis's novel for the screen felt the need to insert a narrative device to give unity and purpose to the novel's discrete adventures. In so doing they stayed true to the Jason-and-the-Argonauts spirit of the book while missing out on much of its underlying message.

Trials and Tribulations

Both novel and film begin when the two younger Pevensie siblings, Edmund and Lucy, together with their obnoxious, imagination-deprived cousin Eustace Clarence Scrubb, are transported, via a magic painting, into Narnia. Once there, they join King Caspian and the crew of the *Dawn Treader* as they search for the seven lords.

As in the two previous films, the screenwriters do a fine job developing the inner conflicts and emotions of the children *before* they enter Narnia: Edmund, like his brother Peter in *Prince Caspian*, cannot get used to the real, mundane world after having been a king and makes a failed attempt to join the British army; Lucy, older and a bit less misty-eyed, struggles with being less pretty than her sister Susan and briefly imagines herself as a glamour girl in love with a soldier; Eustace sports a room full of bugs in bottles and bemoans the fact that he cannot confine his cousins to bottles as well. These snapshot characterizations set up the children, and the audience, for the many temptations they will face during their journey.

Indeed, in working out these temptations the film proves itself to be both faithful and unfaithful to the novel. I said a moment ago that the novel is episodic and loosely organized, but that is only partly true. Behind the archetypal quest for lost lords lies a far deeper unifying device that hearkens back to Bunyan's *Pilgrim's Progress*. Caspian, the three children, and Reepicheep the talking mouse—who matures from the devil-may-care warrior of *Prince Caspian* to a Sir Galahad-like knight whose courage is matched by his purity of heart and who joins the crew in hope of reaching Aslan's Country—are less soldiers of fortune in search of adventure than pilgrims on the road to illumination.

Though Aristotle, and, after him, Hollywood, preferred tightly-constructed plots with a rising action that culminates with a single climax, life—in particular, the *spiritual* life—rarely organizes itself in such a way. We do not conquer one terrible foe in a moment of triumph and then sail on smoothly with nary a ripple. Rather, like the protagonist of Bunyan's allegory, we face a series of small and medium-sized trials that test our courage, our faith, and our resolve.

To survive, we need not combine the strength of Samson with the wisdom of Solomon; we need only rest on the promise of God's provision: "There hath no temptation taken you but such as is common to man: but God is faithful, who will not suffer you to be tempted above that ye are able; but will with the temptation also make a way to escape, that ye may be able to bear it" (1 Corinthians 10:13, KJV). Though Aslan is, as Lewis himself made clear, the Christ of Narnia—he is what the Second Person of the Trinity might have been like had he incarnated himself on a magic world of talking animals and living trees—in *The Voyage of the Dawn Treader* he more often takes on the role of the Holy Spirit: guiding, comforting, and protecting the heroes through their tribulations.

The Green Mist

On the simplest level, the filmmakers understand this aspect of the novel. While preserving all of the major episodes, they rearrange them in such a way as to fit a plot device straight out of the old Ray Harryhausen Sinbad films. Each of the seven lords, we learn, possesses a magic sword; only by gathering all the swords and laying them down on Aslan's Table can the crew stop an evil green mist before it takes over the islands of the Eastern Sea and, we presume, Narnia itself.

Given the fact that our heroes stumble on to the swords, rather than employ strength or wit to acquire them, the collect-the-swords cliché is serviceable at best. It provides a backdrop for some swashbuckling sword fights, well-chosen island locales, sweeping cinematography, magical special effects, an excellent CGI dragon and sea serpent, and a first-rate ship. However, with the exception of the final scene in which Eustace fights to get the seventh sword on to the Table, the finding of the seven swords proves as uninteresting, uneventful, and anti-climactic as the finding of Lewis's seven lords.

The green mist is far more promising. *The Voyage of the Dawn Treader* is the only one of the Chronicles that lacks a central villain; the milquetoast Governor Gumpas of the Lone Islands, wisely left out of the film, hardly qualifies. While staying true to the novel's forgoing of a White Witch or Uncle Miraz, the film cleverly embodies the *spirit* of evil in the amorphous green mist that wraps itself around its victims and feeds on their pride, lust, guilt, and fear.

The mist helps visualize the way sin corrupts the mind, seduces the heart, and hypnotizes the will. Though, as I shall argue below, the film continually shies away from the deeper Christian meanings of the novel, the mist powerfully anchors the film within a good vs. evil matrix that prevents it from drifting downward into ethical relativism or postmodern inclusivism.

In the novel, the crew faces a mysterious island shrouded in darkness where one's dreams and nightmares take bodily form. The film has the green mist emanate from this island, thus suggesting, quite profoundly, that there is a link between our darkest fears and the temptation to sin. Hitchcock taught us that the experience of vertigo combines, paradoxically, the fear of falling and the desire to fall. In the same way, the mesmerizing mist forces Caspian and Edmund to face the two people they both yearn to and shrink from meeting.

The former, desperate to live up to the high reputation of his late father (also King Caspian), struggles throughout the film with his inadequacies as successor. He wants to please him, to be a strong and just ruler, but he simultaneously worries that his father would be disappointed with him. Edmund, meanwhile, has never forgotten the White Witch's promise to make him High King; he despises the Witch, yet a part of him is as desperate as Caspian to prove his worth and his courage—to be braver than Peter, as Lucy is tempted to be prettier than Susan. The mist enables them to meet Father and Witch and, by so doing, forces them to choose the path of good or evil.

As in the novel, Caspian and Edmund also face off over the possession of a magic pool that turns all it touches into gold; however, the film's use of green mist, Father, and Witch makes the struggle over the pool more powerful, by linking it both to pride and fear and to the false pressures and expectations we heap upon ourselves. Alas, the film defuses the struggle by the pool through the intervention of Lucy rather than, as in the novel, through a Holy Spirit-like apparition of Aslan, but the ethical nature of the struggle is preserved and even enhanced.

The film also does a fine job resolving the inner wrestling of Caspian and Edmund. In the final, intensely moving scene—when the main characters meet Aslan on a naked beach beside a frozen wave that marks the barrier between Narnia and Aslan's Country—both young men gain insight into themselves and their capacity for good and evil. Edmund, together with Lucy, realizes that it is time for him to go back home and be a normal boy, rather than a mythic king. This alters the novel, where it is Aslan who tells the despairing siblings that they are too old and cannot return to Narnia, but the change works, for it proceeds from within Edmund and his sister and is faithful to the maturation process that is central to all of Lewis's Chronicles.

Caspian has a similar epiphany. Aslan gives him permission to walk through the wave and be with his father—that is, go to heaven—but if he does, he will not be able to return to Narnia and his throne. He is tempted to do so, but then realizes that his true place is in Narnia, leading the kingdom he fought so hard to win. The scene is a good one—though, in typical American fashion, Caspian, like Edmund, figures out the truth on his own rather than having Aslan reveal it to him—but it lacks the richer dimensions of the parallel scene in the novel.

In Lewis's telling, Caspian, still aboard the *Dawn Treader,* announces to his crew that he is leaving them to sail, along with Reepicheep, to the World's End and gives them instructions on how to choose a new king if he does not return. This is what he *wants* to do, but the crew set him in his place by explaining to him that he is a monarch, not a private person, and that he cannot make decisions simply to please himself. Caspian gets angry, even looking, for a moment, like his uncle Miraz, but he is rebuked by Aslan and submits. Living as we do in an age, and country, that understands little to nothing of the true and sacred duties of kingship, it is a shame that the filmmakers rob us of the medieval Christian lesson that Lewis hoped to teach his young, and not-so-young, readers.

The Magician's Book

True to the novel, the film spends more time developing Lucy's struggles and growth than those of her brother—though the film focuses nearly all of its attention on Lucy's envy of Susan's greater physical beauty. While flipping through a book of incantations, Lucy comes upon a spell that will make her as pretty as Susan. As in the novel, Aslan prevents her from reading the spell, but the film adds a new twist—Lucy rips the spell out of the book for later use—and a new scene—back on board the *Dawn Treader,* Lucy says the spell.

In a lovely use of film magic, Lucy, after saying the spell, walks through a mirror into a gleamingly photographed WWII dance filled with dashing gentlemen and lovely ladies. Lucy now *is* Susan. She is met by Edmund and Peter who take her arms and direct her toward the handsome soldier that the real Susan is dating. Lucy is elated, until she realizes that by getting her wish to be Susan, she (Lucy) no longer exists and, as a result, Peter, Edmund, and the new Lucy-Susan know nothing of Narnia, since it was Lucy who first discovered the entrance to it in the Wardrobe.

Realizing the consequences of her being Susan, Lucy rejects this alternate reality and returns to the ship; whereupon, Aslan appears in the mirror to tell her that she must accept herself for who and what she is. This message is later reinforced through an added character, a young girl from the Lone Islands who stows away on board when her father joins the crew in hope of rescuing his wife from the green mist. The girl quickly comes to idolize Lucy with the same fervor that Lucy feels toward Susan. In a fit of admiration for Lucy, the girl tells her she wants to be just like her when she grows up. Lucy, who has learned the importance of being herself, tells the girl that when she grows up, she should strive to be like herself.

It is a sweet message, and a very American one, but it does a disservice to the deeper ethical lessons taught by Lewis. Let's face it: the youth of America hardly need to be told again that Polonius's bombastic advice ("to thy ownself be true") marks the be all and end all of virtue. It's a good thing that Eustace Clarence Scrubb does not take this advice! How much better and more meaningful the film would have been had it trusted in the power of Lewis's ethical vision and allowed Lucy to have her full interaction with the magician's book.

True, the film does a stunning job making not only the Dufflepuds but the entire house of the magician Coriakin invisible. It also provides us with good special effects for the book and its spells, even adding a spell by which Lucy, quite delightfully, causes it to snow in the room. But there the "improvements" end. In the film, the snow spell gives way to the beautifying spell, and then proceeds directly to Lucy's saying of the spell to make invisible things visible.

In the novel, Lucy, *before* saying the beautifying spell, sees what will happen if she says it: not that she will become Susan and eradicate her own existence, but that she will become another Helen of Troy or Guinevere, causing a war between brave knights who fight for her beauty. With great insight into the nature of temptation and sin, Lewis has Lucy exclaim that she *will* say the spell and that she does *not care*. He then explains—in a simple but profound burst of Christian discernment that the film never achieves—that the reason Lucy said this was because she *knew* that she should not say the spell.

Aslan thankfully prevents her from saying the spell, but Lucy, her egocentric wishes rebuked by the Lion, immediately follows her good choice, not to say the spell, with a bad and willful one. When she turns the page, she comes upon a spell that will allow her to hear what her friends are saying about her. Normally, Lewis tells us, the sensible Lucy would not have said it, but she is in a foul mood for having had her wrongful desire to say the earlier spell curbed, and so she quickly says this one. (In a second instance of fine ethical discernment, Lewis tells us that Lucy said it quickly so as not to give herself time to change her mind.) The images on the book shift, and Lucy finds herself looking on as a friend of hers is prodded by a bully into saying something negative about Lucy. In a huff, Lucy curses the little traitor and turns the page.

Later, when she sees Aslan—who was beside her during her entire ordeal with the magician's book, but who does not become visible until she speaks the visibility spell—Lucy is gently but firmly rebuked for eavesdropping on her friend. Lucy justifies herself by saying it was magic, to which Aslan replies that eavesdropping is eavesdropping no matter the method. He then tells her that the friend she saw in the book really does love her but said bad things out of fear of the bully. Lucy replies that she knows that but that she does not think she can ever forget hearing her friend say those bad things . . . to which Aslan replies that she never will!

Yes, Aslan forgives Lucy for her sin of eavesdropping, but he makes sure that she understands that her bad choices have consequences that cannot be escaped—something, incidentally, that does *not* happen when Lucy, in the film, says the spell that transforms her into Susan. "You mean," cries Lucy in the novel, "that if I hadn't said the spell, we would have been best friends forever." "Did I not tell you once before," Aslan replies sadly, "that no one is ever told what would have happened?" The "once before" is a reference to a scene in *Prince Caspian* that was included in the film version. Given the unnecessary burden that the filmmakers have placed upon themselves to make as many cross-references as possible between the films, one would imagine that they would have kept this vital ethical link between *Prince Caspian* and *The Voyage of the Dawn Treader*. But they do not, and a rare chance to present American youth and adults with a mature meditation on ethical decision making is lost.

And something else is lost as well. After saying the eavesdropping spell, Lucy comes upon a spell for the refreshment of the spirit. The spell is really a story that Lucy does not so much read as experience. Lewis does not explain the exact nature of the story—though he gives clues that reveal it as a cross between the Gospel story and the Holy Grail—but he tells us that it is the most beautiful story Lucy ever read and that it stays with her—not the details, which fade away, but the feeling they provoke—for the rest of her life. Moved by the story, Lucy tries to turn back the pages to read it again. That's when she finds that the book is like life itself: you can only turn the pages forward, never backward.

Is this message not a stronger and more pressing one than the clichéd "be yourself," and would it not have fit in nicely with the film's focus on making wise choices? How wonderful it would have been to see this scene visualized, and how much more wonderful if the film had included as well the promise Aslan makes to Lucy at the end of the episode that someday he will tell her the story again and again.

And, if I may be allowed one last detail from the magician's book episode that the film leaves out. When Aslan becomes visible and Lucy sees him, for a moment, Lewis tells us, she looks, though she does not know it, as beautiful as the beautified Lucy in the book. What a strong message that tiny detail could have sent to Americans of all ages who do not know how to relate internal beauty to external. Unlike the reprehensible ending of *Shrek*, where the princess stays an ogre (thus teaching us that external beauty is meaningless), this scene, if only it had found its way into the film, would have taught its audience that we only find our true beauty when we reflect Christ, the one who created and died to save us.

The Un-dragoning of Eustace

Although the actors who play Lucy and Edmund seem slightly less easy in their roles than in the first two films, and though Ben Barnes's Caspian is less charismatic than in the previous film, the actor who plays Eustace is spot on. He realizes the many dimensions of his character with great relish, and the audience is allowed to be annoyed by him without ever quite hating him.

Perhaps the finest aspect of the film is the way the writers and director carefully modulate and develop the relationship between the spoiled and cowardly Eustace and the bold and chivalrous Reepicheep, who is even better voiced and animated than he was in *Prince Caspian*. In fact, it is from Reepicheep that the audience learns the proper way to view and treat Eustace: not as a monster but as a potentially noble soul struggling to escape from layers of narcissism and ill breeding. In that sense, of course, Eustace is like all of us—made in God's image, and therefore capable of great courage and self-sacrifice, but fallen, and therefore rebellious, disobedient, and self-serving at heart.

Reepicheep's attempts to teach Eustace the rudiments of good behavior are both funny and touching, and the screen springs to life when Reepicheep challenges Eustace to an exciting and marvelously choreographed duel which he uses as a hands-on classroom. By the end of the duel, we sense that Eustace's hatred of Reepicheep has evolved into a cautious respect that has poked holes in, but not eradicated, his spiteful and peevish nature. Still, despite Reepicheep's patient tutelage, the film, in keeping with the novel, makes clear that Eustace's change of heart will necessitate far more drastic measures: namely, Eustace's transformation into a dragon.

On the one hand, I was disappointed that the film discarded the lengthy passage during which Eustace learns that he is a dragon. In the novel, Eustace, for ten long and terrifying minutes, thinks he is sleeping and then crawling beside a dragon—that is, until he realizes that he *is* the dragon. This scene is vital both psychologically and ethically, for it mimics the way sin slowly transforms us into something less than human. It also suggests an analogy between Eustace's condition and the plight of biblical lepers, whose disease the Old Testament treats as an outward manifestation in the flesh of how sin corrupts and blisters the soul.

On the other, I must concede that this would have slowed down the film and prevented the filmmakers from carrying off a truly thrilling recognition scene. Since we, like the crew of the *Dawn Treader*, do not know that the dragon who suddenly appears on screen and seems to attack the ship is Eustace, we share in the shock, relief, and bewilderment when we learn the true identity of the dragon. And what a memorably cinematic way to effect this recognition: by having the dragon pluck Edmund off the ship, lift him high up over the island, and show him burnt out across a vast stretch of sand the letters "I AM EUSTACE." That is filmmaking at its finest!

Unfortunately, no such cinematic justification is apparent for the decision to severely cut back the absolutely central scene in which Eustace is un-dragoned. Although, near the end of the film, Eustace fills in some of the action left out of the un-dragoning scene, it does not suffice. In the film, we see the dragon scratch himself once, and then Aslan drags his claws across the sand, causing a tear to cut across the dragon and the dragon skin to disappear. Now, Aslan digging his claws into the sand makes for a strong visual image, but it is essential that we see, as we do in the novel, Eustace make several attempts to *take off* his dragon skin.

We need to see Eustace rip off his hideous dragon scales like a snake casting off its skin, only to have him realize a moment later that he is still a dragon. And we need to see at least one more attempt, followed by a sense of utter despair on the part of Eustace. Then, we must hear Aslan make his offer to the desperate boy: "Will you let *me* undress you?", followed by Eustace's acceptance of the offer. What Lewis is trying to do here is quite plain. Just as the death and resurrection of Aslan in *The Lion, the Witch and the Wardrobe* reenacts in Narnia the events of Good Friday and Easter, so the un-dragoning of Eustace offers an allegory for the process by which one is "born again"—that is, participates in the death and resurrection of the Second Person of the Trinity.

To drive home the link, Lewis follows the un-dragoning with an actual baptism, in which Aslan throws the born-again Eustace into a well. To be more precise, the scene *begins* with Aslan telling the dragon to wash in the well, prompting Eustace's realization that he must undress (shed the Old Man, as Paul would say) before he can enter the cool, soothing water—a prospect that fills the dragon with desire, for the arm bracelet (representative of original sin) that he cannot remove is cutting into his dragon skin and causing him great pain. The film includes the arm bracelet, but then destroys its meaning by having Lucy easily remove it from the dragon!

I am aware that I may sound like a nit-picker in insisting that this scene should have been visualized in the film, but I believe the criticism is justified by the centrality of the scene to both the dramatic and ethical framework of the novel (and film!). In the life-long struggle to resist temptation and choose the path of good over evil, there must come a time when we realize our ultimate inadequacy and turn to divine aid—as Lucy does in both the novel and film when she calls on Aslan to rescue them from the dark island/green mist.

The loss of Lewis's nuanced and richly theological un-dragoning scene is profound; nevertheless, it must be conceded that the scene in which Reepicheep comforts the dragon with stories of his famous exploits is even more powerful in the film than it is in the book. While most of the crew sleeps nervously on the *Dawn Treader*, Caspian, Lucy, Edmund, and Reepicheep camp out on the beach with the lonely Eustace under a breath-taking canopy of stars. The camaraderie between the five main characters as they huddle together for protection against their physical and spiritual foes is palpable, and we cannot help but feel a rush of love for the kind and noble Reepicheep as he lifts the spirits of the despondent Eustace.

Reepicheep's Journey into Light

Let me say again that the seven swords plus green mist narrative device that the film uses to unify the novel's discrete adventures works well on the whole and keeps the plot moving at a rapid, actually, too rapid, pace. But it comes at a great cost. Aside from the damage done to the magician's book episode and the un-drag-oning of Eustace, the new plot structure forces the sacrifice of the most haunting and mystical part of the book: the meeting with Ramandu followed by the voyage east to the borders of Aslan's country. The exciting climax that brings together the defeat of the sea serpent with the placing of the seventh sword on Aslan's Table prevents the film from devoting more than ten minutes to the last three chapters of the novel.

Though we meet Ramandu's daughter, we do not meet Ramandu himself, nor do we see the birds that fly daily to his island to devour the uneaten food on Aslan's Table. The deep magic of Ramandu and the sacramental nature of the Table are lost as is the numinous scene in which one of the birds places a fire-berry in Ramandu's mouth (patterned after Isaiah 6:6-7). Nor do we learn that Ramandu is a retired star, and that the purpose of the berries is to slowly rejuvenate him until he may re-ascend to the heavens to take his part in the Great Dance of the cosmos.

And because we do not learn this, we lose one of the fin-est lines in all of literature, a line that cuts to the very core of the problem with Eustace and the modern world of which he is a product. When Eustace learns the true identity of Ramandu, he exclaims that in our world, a star is nothing but a flaming ball of gas. But Ramandu corrects him: "no," he says, "even in your world that is not what a star is, but only what it is made of."

If only the film could have preserved this line: if only it could have prodded the audience to reexamine their uncritical belief that to know the physical make up of something—whether that something be a star, a mouse, or a man—is to know its essence, its meaning, and its purpose. We share Eustace's arrogant belief that all of life can be catalogued like bugs in bottles and that empirical science can somehow explain who and what we are as human beings. The film *does* show that Eustace has read all the wrong books and that his rejection of fairy tales has left him stunted and even unprotected, but it does not show that his limited vision is that of our own technological, mechanistic age.

And then there is the final journey into light, a journey that conveys much of the wonder and awe of Dante's journey through paradise to the Empyrean of God. The film includes the prophecy spoken over the young Reepicheep that he will one day reach the utter east, the sign of which will be that sky and water will meet and the waves will grow sweet. But the prophecy is inserted in such a quick and offhanded manner that the audience misses the words.

Worse yet, when Reepicheep cries out that the water is sweet, the filmmakers do not bother to explain that what has happened is that the salt ocean has suddenly, and miraculously, turned into a fresh (or sweet) water river. In any case, it all happens so quickly that the audience is lost. One second they have escaped from the dark island; the next second Reepicheep is shouting that the water is sweet. A few seconds later, the water is filled with lilies—a phenomenon that is not even commented on!—and then they are there with Aslan on the beach beside the frozen wave.

One thing I specialize in is epic literature, and I can attest to the fact that the voyage from Ramandu's island to the sea of lilies is joyously and stirringly wonderful beyond belief. As in Dante's *Paradiso*, our heroes journey into greater and greater light, until it becomes almost too much too bear. But then they drink of the "sweet" water, and it is as if they have drunk liquid light. Now they can stare directly into the sun—like eagles, says Lewis, in keeping with the medieval belief that the eyes of eagles were so pure they could gaze into the sun—and need no further nourishment.

The filmmakers preserve Reepicheep's final voyage up the wave into Aslan's Country and preserve as well Aslan's assurance that he also exists in our world but that there he goes by another name. For these things they are to be highly commended. But we miss out on the fullness of Aslan's final explanation—that to get from our world to Aslan's Country we must cross a great river (the river Jordan, or death, in biblical allegory), but that we need not fear, for he is the great bridge builder. Well, maybe the Christology here was just too strong for Hollywood, but the image of the river and the bridge are such rich archetypes that their inclusion would have strengthened the overall imagery and resonance of the film.

Still, despite leaving out much of what makes *The Voyage of the Dawn Treader* a book to treasure and contemplate, the film nevertheless remains faithful to the adventures and the characters that go on them. It offers a journey well worth taking, and I hope it will revive the kind of sea-faring swashbucklers that fired my own imagination as a boy. Rest assured that for all its flaws, the movie has the power to transform the most calculating, left-brained, unimaginative of children into would-be sailors of the high seas. And that, I think, would have pleased C. S. Lewis.

Recommended
Reading

BOOKS BY C. S. LEWIS

In this bibliography, I will suggest an order in which you might want to read the copious and diverse works of C. S. Lewis. Since all of these books exist in numerous editions, I will not attempt to specify one over the other. Any edition will do. After the title of the book, I have given the original date of publication.

Screwtape Letters (1942). This series of letters from a senior devil to a junior devil instructing him in the fine art of tempta- tion is, to my mind, the ideal starting place for a journey through the world of C. S. Lewis. It balances humor with deep spiritual insight in a way that is powerfully engaging. You will find yourself laughing and being convicted at the same time.

The Great Divorce (1946). This timeless fantasy asks itself a provocative question: what if the people in hell were allowed to take a bus ride to heaven and, while there, be met by the souls of saints they knew in life? If those saints gave them the chance, even now, to accept grace and stay in heaven, what would they do? A mixture of theology, philosophy, ethics, and top-notch story-tell- ing, this has always been my single favorite Lewis book. Together with *Screwtape Letters*, it explores the psychology of sin and the reality of grace in a winsome way.

Mere Christianity (1952). After reading *Screwtape* and *Great Divorce*, you are ready to take up Lewis's single greatest work of Christian apologetics. In addition to offering powerful arguments in favor of the existence of God and the truth of the gospel, this book explores the nature of Christian morality and defines key Christian doctrines. Rather than base all of his arguments on the Bible (a book that not all moderns accept as inspired), Lewis finds evidence in common human experience for the central teachings of the faith.

The Chronicles of Narnia (1950-56). While you are reading the above three books, you should be working your way through the seven Chronicles. But please, do not read them in the order they are currently published; rather, read them in their original order of publication: *The Lion, the Witch and the Wardrobe, Prince Caspian, The Voyage of the Dawn Treader, The Silver Chair, The Horse and His Boy, The Magician's Nephew,* and *The Last Battle.* Here you will find Lewis at his best, fusing reason and imagination in a manner accessible to all ages.

The Problem of Pain (1940). This was Lewis's first work of apologetics; its success led to his being invited to give the Broadcast Talks that led to *Mere Christianity.* It is filled with insights, not only about the problem of pain, but about creation, Adam and Eve, heaven, and hell.

A Grief Observed (1961). This is the logical follow up to reading *The Problem of Pain.* If that book addresses the topic of pain and suffering in a rational way, *A Grief Observed* takes it up again from an intensely personal point of view. The books complement each other and should be read in close proximity.

The Space Trilogy: *Out of the Silent Planet* (1938), *Perelandra* (1943), *That Hideous Strength* (1945). Though this series may not be to all tastes, it contains some of Lewis's most mature reflections on the nature of God, man, and the universe. The first book is a fast read in the mode of H. G. Wells, but the second and third call for considerable more concentration and effort. Do at least read the second, as it offers a profound reenactment of the fall of man. I know many people who have started the third book many times but didn't finish it. If the same happens to you, don't worry. Put it aside and pick it up at a later date. I do believe it should be read at some point, but don't feel rushed.

Surprised by Joy (1955). OK, if you've come this far, it is time to read Lewis's spiritual autobiography. This is not an easy book, and it delves quite often into some rather arcane ideas, but it is an important book if you really want to get to the soul of C. S. Lewis and to the soul of modernism.

Till We Have Faces (1956). This is not an easy novel to read, but Lewis considered it his finest work of fiction and for good reason. As with *That Hideous Strength*, you may feel the need to put it down for a later date, but do take up the challenge of reading it at some point. It is a unique experience not to be missed.

Reflections on the Psalms (1958), **The Four Loves** (1960), and/or **Letters to Malcolm** (1964). These are slightly lesser-known Lewis works, but they are accessible and take up aspects of the Christian life not covered in his other books. Save them for a rainy day.

Miracles (1947). This is the most difficult of Lewis's apologetical books, but it is still very timely and offers its reader a fresh new way of looking at the supernatural in general and miracles in particular. Don't be intimated by chapter three; just skim it and then move on to chapter four.

The Abolition of Man (1943). Thus far, I have not mentioned any of Lewis's academic works. If you feel ready to take up this aspect of Lewis's work, this is the book to start with. It is an amazingly prophetic book on the dangers of a modern, values-free education. This is a must read for all educators. In fact, if you are a teacher, you should move this to the top of the list. This book should be read in conjunction with *That Hideous Strength*.

A Preface to Paradise Lost (1942). I think this is the most accessible of Lewis's books on literature and aesthetic history. It offers thoughtful analysis, not only of Milton's epic, but of the *Iliad*, *Odyssey*, *Aeneid*, and *Beowulf*. It is an important work because it countered the romantic temptation to treat Satan as the true hero of *Paradise Lost*. This book should be read in conjunction with *The Problem of Pain* and *Perelandra*.

The Discarded Image (1964). This is my favorite of Lewis's academic works, for it lays out in beautiful detail the medieval model of the cosmos around which Dante constructed his *Divine Comedy*. It gets technical at points, but it is still accessible on the whole.

An Experiment in Criticism (1961). I have found that this brief work, in which Lewis lays out an intriguing theory about the nature of reading, has strong appeal to non-humanities people.

Here are four other works by Lewis that, though they contain real gems, are often hard for the common reader to get through: ***The Pilgrim's Regress*** (1933), ***The Allegory of Love*** (1936), ***English Literature in the Sixteenth Century*** (1954), and ***Studies in Words*** (1960).

As for the many collections out there of Lewis's essays, the ones that are the most accessible are ***God in the Dock*** (includes Lewis's best short reflections on miracles, nature, apologetics, and myth), ***The Weight of Glory*** (the title essay and "Transpositions" offer profound studies of heaven; "The Inner Ring" and "Membership" are central to Lewis's thought), ***On Stories*** (includes seminal essays on children's literature, fairy tales, and science fiction), ***Selected Literary Essays*** (includes the talk Lewis gave when he accepted the Chair of Medieval and Renaissance Literature at Cambridge, along with free-standing essays on Chaucer, Shakespeare, Bunyan, Austen, Shelley, Scott, Morris, and Kipling), and **Christian Reflections** (explores the relationship between literature, culture, and Christianity).

Lewis was an avid letter writer, and his letters are filled with timeless insight. Lewis's **Collected Letters** are available in three thick volumes.

BOOKS ABOUT C. S. LEWIS

With each passing year, more and more books on C. S. Lewis appear in bookstores and online. Here are some standard studies that I have found both useful and accessible.

Carpenter, Humphrey. *The Inklings: C. S. Lewis, J. R. R. Tolkien, Charles Williams, and Their Friends*. Boston: Houghton Mifflin, 1979. Well-conceived, well-documented "collective biography."

Como, James T. C. S. *Lewis at the Breakfast Table and Other Reminiscences*. New York: Macmillan, 1979. Offers a smorgasbord of essays written by those who knew Lewis best.

Dorsett, Lyle W. *And God Came In: The Extraordinary Story of Joy Davidman, Her Life and Marriage to C. S. Lewis*. New York: Macmillan, 1983. Best overall account of Lewis's marriage to Joy.

Downing, David C. *Planets in Peril: A Critical Study of C. S. Lewis's Ransom Trilogy*. Amherst: University of Massachusetts Press, 1992. Best one-volume study of The Space Trilogy; boasts extensive bibliography.

Duriez, Colin. *Tolkien and C. S. Lewis: The Gift of Friendship*. Mahwah, NJ: HiddenSpring, 2003. Good standard study of this vital friendship.

Ford, Paul F. *Companion to Narnia*. San Francisco: Harper & Row, 1980. Fans of the Chronicles must own this book; it offers an encyclopedia of all the characters, places, and themes of Narnia.

Glyer, Diana. *The Company They Keep: C. S. Lewis and J. R. R. Tolkien as Writers in Community*. Kent, OH: Kent State University Press, 2008. Fine study of the Inklings in action.

Hooper, Walter. *C. S. Lewis: A Companion and Guide*. San Francisco: Harper & Row, 1996. One of the best available resources by one who understands Lewis as an editor, friend and critic.

Jacobs, Alan. *The Narnian: The Life and Imagination of C. S. Lewis*. San Francisco: HarperSan Francisco, 2005. Though I still prefer Sayer's biography, this one is very strong on links to Narnia and is well written, with good use of Lewis's letters.

Kreeft, Peter. *C. S. Lewis for the Third Millennium: Six Essays on 'The Abolition of Man.'* San Francisco: Ignatius Press, 1994. Fine study that considers from hindsight the accuracy of Lewis's predictions.

Martin, Thomas L., ed. *Reading the Classics with C. S. Lewis*. Grand Rapids, MI: Baker, 2000. This excellent collection of essays takes up Lewis's interactions with authors, literary periods, and genres. It also provides an intimate glimpse of Lewis in the classroom and the library.

McGrath. Alister. *C. S. Lewis: A Life*. Carol Stream, IL: Tyndale, 2013. One of the most balanced and well-researched biographies of Lewis available, this book brings to life every phase in Lewis's education, teaching career, and scholarship.

Meilaender, Gilbert. *The Taste for the Other: The Social and Ethical Thought of C. S. Lewis*. Grand Rapids: Eerdmans, 1978. Brilliant, sensitive study with much to say on the Space Trilogy.

Nicholi, Armand, Jr. *The Question of God: C. S. Lewis and Freud Debate God, Love, Sex, and the Meaning of Life.* New York: Free Press, 2002. A brilliant comparative analysis that contrasts opposing worldviews. It was later turned into a PBS series and inspired a one-act play, *Freud's Last Session.*

Piper, John and David Mathis, eds. *The Romantic Rationalist: God, Life, and Imagination in the Work of C. S. Lewis.* Wheaton, IL: Crossway Books, 2014. A thought-provoking collection of essays from a Reformed perspective that takes up Lewis's views on scripture, Calvinism, and salvation.

Sayer, George. *Jack: A Life of C. S. Lewis.* Wheaton, IL: Crossway Books, 1994. An excellent biography by a one-time pupil and long-time friend that combines personal insight with critical objectivity.

Schakel, Peter J. *Reason and Imagination in C. S. Lewis: A Study of 'Till We Have Faces.'* Grand Rapids: Eerdmans, 1984. The definitive study of Lewis's strangest and most haunting novel.

Sibley, Brian. *The Land of Narnia: Brian Sibley Explores the World of C. S. Lewis.* New York: HarperCollins, 1989. A simple book that can be enjoyed by children and their parents alike.

Vaus, Will. *Mere Theology: A Guide to the Thought of C. S Lewis.* Downers Grove, IL: Very accessible overview of Lewis's thought on a number of issues from Creation and Fall to faith and morality to the person and work of Christ to the Trinity.

Ward, Michael. *Planet Narnia: The Seven Heavens in the Imagination of C. S. Lewis.* New York: Oxford University Press, 2008; reissued as *The Narnia Code.* A brilliant, fresh reading that argues that Lewis keyed each Chronicle to the seven medieval planets.

Werther, David and Susan. C. S. *Lewis's List: The Ten Books that Influenced Him Most*. New York: Bloomsbury Academic, 2015. Ten Lewis scholars look at the ten books that Lewis, near the end of his life, said had exerted the strongest influence on him. They include books by Wordsworth, Chesterton, Charles Williams, George MacDonald, Boethius, and George Herbert. I myself contributed the chapter on Virgil's *Aeneid*.

Williams, Rowan. *The Lion's World: A Journey into the Heart of Narnia*. Oxford: Oxford University Press, 2012. A brief, heartfelt study by the former Archbishop of Canterbury.

A LIST OF MY OWN
BOOKS ON C. S. LEWIS

C. S. Lewis: An Apologist for Education (Classical Academic Press, 2015)

In addition to being one of the great apologists and writers of the last century, Lewis was a prescient observer of education and a thoughtful critic of modern educational theory and practice. In this brief book, I survey Lewis's thought on education as represented in such books as *The Abolition of Man*, *An Experiment in Criticism*, *The Discarded Image*, and the *Collected Letters*. I seek to offer a timely call to renew a radical liberal arts education that assumes a meaningful, purposeful cosmos and that will awaken students "from the slumber of cold vulgarity" and cultivate their affections for truth, goodness, and beauty.

On The Shoulders of Hobbits: The Road to Virtue with Tolkien and Lewis (Moody, 2012)

This book seeks to revive a more traditional understanding of virtue and vice and of human purpose and dignity by analyzing closely Lewis's Chronicles of Narnia and Tolkien's Lord of the Rings. Each chapter takes up a single theme (the nature of pilgrimage, facing death, kingship and hierarchy, the virtue of hope, the love that forgives, forbidden fruit) that has been overlooked or dismissed by our age, and then illustrates and embodies that theme by reference to these two great works of fantasy.

Apologetics for the 21st Century (Crossway, 2010)

This book surveys the work of the finest popular apologists of the last century—Lewis, Chesterton, Schaeffer, McDowell, Strobel, Zacharias, and Wright among them—who have successfully demonstrated not only that Christianity "makes sense" but that it has the power to explain the nature of God, man, and the universe. Six chapters are devoted to Lewis.

Restoring Beauty: The Good, the True, and the Beautiful in the Writings of C. S. Lewis (IVP, 2010)

More and more in our modern and postmodern culture, beauty and truth have been separated both from each other and from their individual connection to a divine source of Beauty and Truth. As both an effective apologist for truth-based education and as a sub-creator of his own beauty-enhancing fiction, C. S. Lewis is the ideal guide for all those who would seek to restore truth and beauty to their proper place and role in our world.

Lewis Agonistes: How C. S. Lewis Can Train Us to Wrestle with the Modern and Postmodern World (Broadman & Holman, 2003)

In this book, I survey the life and major fictional and non-fictional works of C. S. Lewis in such a way as to empower readers to wrestle *alongside* Lewis as he takes on the challenges of the modern and postmodern world. After a mini-biography of Lewis that explores the life experiences that helped form him into the great wrestler he was, I take up five of the most controversial issues of our day: 1) science, 2) the New Age, 3) evil and suffering, 4) the arts and postmodernism, and 5) heaven and hell.

The Life and Writings of C. S. Lewis (The Teaching Company/Great Courses, 2000)

In this 12-lecture audio series, I offer a full overview of the life and major works of C. S. Lewis. The series comes with a detailed course pack that includes an extensive annotated bibliography.

ADDITIONAL RESOURCES

In addition to the three Hollywood films reviewed above, the first four Chronicles of Narnia have been filmed (in live action) by the BBC as part of the WonderWorks Series (1988). They are good for children and faithful to the books, though a bit stiff and chatty. *The Lion, the Witch, and the Wardrobe* has also been made into a delightful, Emmy Award-winning animated film that I find more compelling than the live-action BBC version.

Best of all, Focus on the Family's Radio Theater has turned all seven Chronicles into excellent radio plays that are faithful to the novels and done with great style. They are introduced by Lewis's stepson, Douglas Gresham, and include the voices of Paul Scofield as the narrator and David Suchet as Aslan. The Chronicles are also available (from Harper Audio) in unabridged audio book format, read by such great British actors as Kenneth Branagh, Patrick Stewart, Michael York, and Derek Jacobi.

The story of Lewis's marriage to Joy Davidman and her subsequent death from cancer is powerfully told in a British made-for-TV movie, *Shadowlands* (1985; also known as *C. S. Lewis: Through the Shadowlands*) that was later expanded into a major motion picture of the same name, directed by Richard Attenborough and starring Anthony Hopkins and Debra Winger (1993). It was also adapted into a fine stage play.

Finally, two DVD collections are available (*The Four Loves*; *C. S. Lewis Speaks His Mind*) that allow the purchaser to hear Lewis speak in his own voice. In the former, Lewis reads an abridged version of *The Four Loves*. In the latter, he gives lectures on *Pilgrim's Progress* and Charles Williams and famously argues that the Renaissance never happened. Both are available from the Episcopal Media Center.

READING IN THE SHADOW OF NARNIA

Though more than half a century has passed since C. S. Lewis published his Chronicles of Narnia, interest in his beloved fantasy books for children continues to increase with each passing year. The reasons for this success are many and diverse, but they would certainly include the following: 1) the talking animals and living trees of Narnia beckon to modern children (and adults) who yearn for a deeper connection with nature; 2) the Christian allegory that underlies the Chronicles not only appeals to Christians seeking a new perspective on their faith but to spiritual seekers who have been "turned off" by the legalism and over-rationalism they have encountered in the church; 3) the numinous power, rich magic, and compassionate heart of Aslan, the Lion King of Narnia, weaves a spell over readers of all ages and backgrounds; 4) the novels help their readers to understand the full nature of good and evil, presenting a moral universe where our choices matter; 5) Narnia is a land that runs on medieval values of hierarchy, order, and honor, values which our modern society often lacks or misunderstands; 6) the novels work on many different levels, offering simple moral lessons for their child readers and more nuanced explorations of virtue and vice for their adult readers.

Once readers have entered Lewis's magical land, they often find themselves hungry for other books that offer an experience similar to that of the Chronicles. In this bibliography, I will survey a number of books written before, during, and after the Chronicles of Narnia that will likely be appreciated, and even savored, by fans of Lewis's work.

• • •

The best place to start is with some of the children's books that the young Lewis read and loved. These would include the lovely *Tales of Beatrix Potter*, whose stories and illustrations often swept Lewis away to a place of joy and enchantment. Potter had an uncanny ability for anthropomorphizing animals while yet allowing them to retain their distinct animal nature: something that Lewis succeeds in doing with the memorable beavers, badgers, owls, and squirrels that populate his Chronicles.

A Lewis favorite that should be read by every child, and reread by every adult, is Kenneth Grahame's *The Wind in the Willows*. Grahame, like Potter, had a gift for endowing his anthropomorphized animals (Mole, Rat, Toad) with eccentricities that are both recognizably human and distinctly animal. In addition, Grahame was able to infuse his children's novels with a kind of spiritual wonder and richness that never become preachy or didactic. In one scene, when Mole and Rat meet the god Pan, Grahame conjures a feeling of numinous power that points forward to Lewis's depiction of Aslan.

Lewis also enjoyed the fantasy tales of E. Nesbitt (*Five Children and It, The Phoenix and the Wishing Carpet, The Amulet*), borrowing from her the precocious, if slightly dated, lingo of her appealing child heroes. Along with these, he also thrilled to the magical lands conjured in Lewis Carroll's *Alice in Wonderland* and *Through the Looking Glass*, the more exotic locales of the *Arabian Nights* and Rudyard Kipling's *Jungle Book*, and the adventurous vistas of H. Rider Haggard's *She* and *King Solomon's Mines*. Other tales that sparked his imagination and his hunger for other worlds include E. R. Eddison's *The Worm*

Ourobos, the medieval and romantic novels of Sir Walter Scott (*Ivanhoe, Waverley*), the Arthurian and fantasy tales of William Morris (especially *The Well at the World's End*), and the Sherlock Holmes stories of Sir Arthur Conan Doyle.

As for fairy tales, Lewis grew up reading the stories collected by Andrew Lang under a series of colorful titles: *The Red Fairy Book, The Blue Fairy Book, The Green Fairy Book*, and so forth. These beautiful books are all available in well-illustrated facsimile editions from Dover Press at a very affordable price; every home with children must have these books on the shelf. They offer the best retellings of classic fairy tales from all over Europe and even more far-flung countries like China and India.

Though Lewis loved Greek and Roman mythology, he loved even more the Norse sagas, particularly Wagner's Ring cycle and its major sources, *The Nibelungenlied* and *The Volsung Saga*. His love for myth and fairy tales also extended to his passion for medieval allegories: *The Faerie Queene, The Romance of the Rose, Piers Plowman, Sir Gawain and The Green Knight, Orlando Furioso, Troilus and Criseyde*, and so forth. Though allegory tends to be less read, and even less appreciated, today than it was in the past, Lewis was an advocate and apologist for these old tales and their ability to work on several levels of meaning.

• • •

George MacDonald, though he lived almost a full century before Lewis, profoundly impacted Lewis's work. He has experienced something of a resurgence over the last several decades, and his books are well worth reading. Younger children will thrill to his *At the Back of the North Wind, The Princess and the Goblin, The Princess and Curdie*, and his many fairy tales (especially "The Light Princess"), but Lewis was most influenced by his dark yet hopeful Christian fantasy novels, *Phantastes* and *Lilith*. Of the former novel, Lewis said that reading it "baptized his imagination." These rich and strange novels are a bit preachier than the Chronicles, but they have a power to open their readers' eyes to new dimensions of reality and to the greater forces that lie all about us.

Charles Williams was a contemporary of Lewis and a member of a writers' group called the Inklings that was started by Lewis and J. R. R. Tolkien. Williams' seven mystical novels lie somewhere between *Phantastes* and the Chronicles. They center around very ordinary characters who are catapulted into a world of spiritual warfare that few people ever experience. The best of the novels, *Descent into Hell*, concerns a suicide seeking redemption, a woman who sees her doppelganger (or "dark other"), a saintly playwright who teaches the woman that she must learn to bear the suffering of others, and a narcissistic man who is in love with a succubus (an evil spirit that takes on the form of a beautiful young woman).

The Place of the Lion, a novel whose Platonic Christian vision foreshadows the last of the Chronicles, wonders what the results would be if the Forms of things suddenly invaded our world. *War in Heaven* takes us along on a modern-day search for the Holy Grail. In addition to his Chronicles, Lewis wrote three science-fiction novels that are generally referred to as The Space Trilogy: *Out of the Silent Planet*; *Perelandra*; *That Hideous Strength*. The third of these novels was directly patterned after the novels of Charles Williams.

Lewis shared a long and close friendship with J. R. R. Tolkien, and his *Hobbit* and The Lord of the Rings (*The Fellowship of the Ring*, *The Two Towers*, *The Return of the King*) are required reading for lovers of the Chronicles. Tolkien's books bring to life, with a depth and breadth of detail that far surpasses the Chronicles, the magical and vivid world of Middle-earth. Tolkien, like Lewis, was a specialist in the field of medieval studies, a linguist of some note, and a lover of Norse mythology, and all these interests find their way into his novels. Some of the first drafts of The Lord of the Rings were read at Inklings meetings, and Lewis himself was one of the first fans and defenders of the trilogy. Though Tolkien shared Lewis's faith, and though his trilogy contains a developed sense of ethics, justice, and morality, it does not attempt to retell the story of Christ or to raise direct issues of faith.

In contrast, Tolkien's The Silmarillion—a collection of tales about the origins of Middle-earth that are told in some of the most beautiful and breath-taking prose ever written—does have much to say on the origin of evil and the nature of Satan, filtered slightly through the Norse god, Loki. Fans of The Lord of the Rings in particular and of fantasy in general should also read Tolkien's definitive book-length essay, "On Fairy-Stories," as well as his shorter tales: "Smith of Wootton Major," "Farmer Giles of Ham," and "Leaf by Niggle."

• • •

Many post-Lewis, post-Tolkien fantasy writers have tried to create fantasy worlds on the grand scale of The Lord of the Rings. My personal favorite is Stephen R. Donaldson's The Chronicles of Thomas Covenant. Though, like The Lord of the Rings, this is not a Christian allegory per se, it creates a fascinating, incredibly complex fantasy world where religious issues abound. It is not meant for young children, but will challenge high school, college, and adult readers.

In the 1990's, Philip Pullman offered the world a self-consciously anti-Narnia trilogy in which Jehovah turns out to be the bad guy! Though well-written and fascinating, His Dark Materials (The Golden Compass, The Subtle Knife, The Amber Spyglass) is guaranteed to upset, and perhaps offend, lovers of the Chronicles. More recently, Lev Grossman's The Magician, The Magician King, and The Magician's Land offer a dark, revisionist reading of the Chronicles (and Harry Potter) that is populated by maladjusted, amoral teenagers. George R. R. Martin's Game of Thrones series is even less appropriate for children, offering graphic sex and violence in a world that has the rich dimensions of The Lord of the Rings but is bereft of a moral center or vision.

More appropriate for younger readers are the novels that make up the Percy Jackson series by Rick Riordan. These embody a truly Lewisian love of mythology and help young readers to wrestle with the nature of choice and the difference between virtue and vice. Of course, these themes are most effectively taken up in the Harry Potter series of J. K. Rowling. Rowling is a great fan of the Chronicles, and, though her novels are not Christian allegories, they embody a traditional, Judeo-Christian understanding of good and evil.

Madeleine L'Engle's *A Wrinkle in Time* and *A Wind in the Door* are wonderful children's books that have a strong spiritual undertone but are never preachy. Her books speak to the child in all of us, drawing out our imagination and our sense of wonder.

Ray Bradbury's *The Martian Chronicles* (a collection of free-standing short stories that are linked thematically) shows the influence of Lewis's The Space Trilogy and often rises to a kind of spiritual allegory that thrills its readers with a numinous awe absent from most twentieth-century literature. Bradbury's many other collections of stories (*The Illustrated Man*, *A Medicine for Melancholy*, etc.) all possess a resonance that is not soon forgotten.

Calvin Miller has written a haunting trilogy that allegorizes the life of Christ and the growth of Christianity: *The Singer*, *The Song*, and *The Finale*. Rendered in a loose, free-flowing verse and accompanied by lovely line drawings, Miller's books exist somewhere between the Chronicles and Bunyan's *Pilgrim's Progress*. Miller has written many other books, some especially for children.

Walter Wangerin's *The Book of the Dun Cow* also possesses a strong allegorical edge that, like the work of Lewis, is indebted to medieval literary forms.

Lewis is a great writer, not only because his books present us with a world that we want to visit again and again, but because they also push us out of that world into the lap of other writers who share Lewis's gift for challenging and captivating audiences of all ages.

ABOUT THE AUTHOR

Louis Markos holds a BA in English and History from Colgate University and an MA and PhD in English from the University of Michigan. He is a Professor of English and Scholar in Residence at Houston Baptist University, where he teaches courses on British Romantic and Victorian Poetry and Prose, the Classics, C. S. Lewis and J. R. R. Tolkien, and Film.

Dr. Markos holds the Robert H. Ray Chair in Humanities and also lectures on Ancient Greece and Rome, the Early Church and Middle Ages, the Renaissance, and Romanticism for HBU's Honors College. He is the author of ten books: *From Achilles to Christ: Why Christians Should Read the Pagan Classics, Pressing Forward: Alfred, Lord Tennyson and the Victorian Age, The Eye of the Beholder: How to See the World like a Romantic Poet, Lewis Agonistes: How C. S. Lewis can Train us to Wrestle with the Modern and Postmodern World*, *Apologetics for the 21ˢᵗ Century, Restoring Beauty: The Good, the True, and the Beautiful in the Writings of C. S. Lewis, Literature: A Student's Guide, On the Shoulders of Hobbits: The Road to Virtue in Tolkien and Lewis, Heaven and Hell: Visions of the Afterlife in the Western Poetic Tradition*, and C. S. *Lewis: An Apologist for Education*. All these books are available at his amazon.com author page: http://www.amazon.com/Louis-Markos.

In addition to books, he has also produced two lecture series with the Teaching Company, *The Life and Writings of*

C. S. Lewis; *Plato to Postmodernism: Understanding the Essence of Literature and the Role of the Author* (available at www. teach12.com), and published over 100 articles and reviews in such journals as *Christianity Today, Touchstone, Theology Today, Christian Research Journal, Mythlore, Christian Scholar's Review, Saint Austin Review, American Arts Quarterly,* and *The City.* Further, his modern adaptation of Euripides' *Iphigenia in Tauris,* Euripides' *Helen,* and Sophocles' *Electra* were performed off-Broadway in the Fall of 2011, Fall of 2012, and Spring of 2013, respectively.

He is a popular speaker and has spoken on such topics as C. S. Lewis, J. R. R. Tolkien, apologetics, Christianity and Education, Ancient Greece, Ancient Rome, Romanticism, and Dante in two dozen states and in Canada, Oxford, and Rome. He is committed to the concept of the Professor as Public Educator and believes that knowledge must not be walled up in the Academy but must be disseminated to all who have ears to hear. He lives in Houston with his wife, Donna, his son, Alex, and his daughter, Stacey.

For more information, and to read his posts, visit his website at: www.Loumarkos.com